Invisible Storytellers

Invisible Storytellers

Voice-Over Narration in
American Fiction Film

Sarah Kozloff

University of California Press
Berkeley / Los Angeles / London

University of California Press
Berkeley and Los Angeles

University of California Press, Ltd.
London, England

© 1988 by
The Regents of the University of California

Library of Congress Cataloging-in-Publication Data

Kozloff, Sarah.
  Invisible storytellers.

  Filmography: p.
  Bibliography: p.
  Includes index.
  1. Moving-picture plays—History and criticism.
2. Moving-pictures—United States.   3. Narration
(Rhetoric)   I. Title: Voice-over narration in American
fiction film.   II. Title.
PN1995.K69   1988   791.43′0973   87-12461
ISBN 0-520-05861-5 (alk. paper)

Printed in the United States of America

1   2   3   4   5   6   7   8   9

To my brother, Daniel Kozloff,
who used to read me stories
and take me to movies

Contents

Acknowledgments

Many people contributed to this study by recommending films with voice-over, suggesting sources, checking out books, or just by their encouraging interest. To all, I am grateful.

Some people's assistance, however, deserves particular mention.

First, since this work's original incarnation was as a doctoral dissertation at Stanford University, I wish to thank my committee for their guidance: my adviser, David Halliburton, and my readers, William Mills Todd III and Henry Breitrose.

Secondly, thanks are due to those who gave me access to the films: William K. Everson, who opened his personal collection to me, and the staffs of the film study centers of the Department of Cinema Studies at New York University, the Museum of Modern Art, and the Library of Congress. I am also grateful to Virginia Clark, Cathy Holter, and Joyce Jesionowski for their assistance with the frame enlargements.

A number of film professionals graciously took the time to answer my queries, among them the screenwriters Philip Dunne and Malvin Wald and editors Barbara McLean, Ralph Rosenblum, and Denise Sickinger.

In addition, I must express a particular debt to those who read portions of the manuscript in draft form, and whose thoughtful suggestions ranged from copyediting to prompting me to rethink the most crucial theoretical issues: Melissa Berman, Nöll Brinckmann, Marian Keane, Susan Ryan, William Rothman, Ian Watt, and—especially—Seymour Chatman. And I have been fortunate indeed in having the most considerate and expert of editors, Ernest Callenbach.

From inception to completion, Leger Grindon and Daniel Kozloff were the ones I turned to with innumerable queries and difficulties. Their contributions cut across all categories.

Finally, no list of thanks would be complete without mention of my husband, Robert Lechterman. He helped in many concrete ways—as consultant, photographer, and courier—but it is for his unequivocal, unflagging support that I am most deeply grateful.

A portion of chapter 4 first appeared in *Cinema Journal* 23, no. 4 (Summer 1984) and is used here with the permission of University of Illinois Press.

Frame enlargements and still photographs are included by courtesy of the following: ABC Pictures International, Inc., Columbia Pictures, Janus Films, the Mark Hellinger Estate, Metro-Goldwyn-Mayer / United Artists, the Museum of Modern Art Film Stills Archive, the New York Public Library for the Performing Arts, Republic Pictures, Twentieth Century–Fox, and Warner Brothers.

Introduction

"Let me tell you a story," each narrative film seems to offer silently as its opening frames hit the screen: "It all started this way . . ."

Behind every film we sense a narrating "voice," a master-of-ceremonies figure that presents and controls the text. But in many cases we also hear from off-screen a human voice—a man, woman, or child who explicitly narrates all or part of the story we are about to witness. In Howard Hawks's *Red River* (1948), an unseen voice (Walter Brennan) remarks:

> You see, the story of the Red River D. started this way. Along about August of 1851 Tom Dunson and me left St. Louie and joined a wagon train headed for Californy. After about three weeks on the trail we was to the northern border of Texas . . .

This prototypical "old-timer" speaks to us as if we were huddled around a campfire on a lonely prairie, not a flickering screen in our neighborhood theater.

Cinematic storytelling is one of the youngest, most technologically dependent, and most expensive modes of narration; oral storytelling, the most ancient, fundamental, and widely accessible. In films with voice-over narration the older form has been superimposed on top of the newer. "Narrated" films are hybrids—almost implying a mixture of centuries and cultures—half-retrograde, half-pathbreaking, half-dissembling, half-forthright, they call upon the viewer to assume complex, if not contradictory, positions. Adding voice-over narration to a film creates a fascinating dance between pose and actuality, word and image, narration and drama, voice and "voice."

Voice-over narration has been a major element of cinema since the thirties; it is so very common that it probably passes the average moviegoer unnoticed. In keeping with the neglect and abhorrence of film sound in general, for too long scholars and critics have also either overlooked the technique or, influenced by various prejudices, dismissed it out of hand. This study seeks to prove that these prejudices are ill-founded and endeavors to remedy this long neglect by tracing the technique's historical development and by analyzing its subtleties, especially its capacity for creating intimacy and sophisticated irony.

In the course of this analysis I draw on the paradigms of recent narrative theorists such as Wayne Booth, Robert Scholes and Robert Kellogg, Roland Barthes, and Gérard Genette, syncretically applying whichever concepts are most relevant to filmic narration in general and voice-over in particular. For the most part, film scholars have heretofore made rather limited use of narrative theory;[1] by the same token, although narrative theorists often make broad claims about the applicability of their discoveries to narrative as a transmedia phenomenon, they habitually and almost exclusively draw their examples from literary texts.[2] By applying "literary" narrative theory to film, I hope both to further our understanding of cinematic narrative's specific characteristics and to test the universality of several key tenets of contemporary critical lore.

I have focused my research on American and British narrative feature films, primarily Hollywood products. Since this field extends over nearly sixty years of sound-film history and encompasses thousands of movies, it is already impractically large, yet even these boundaries exclude important texts from direct consideration. Thus, although documentaries both preceded fiction films in their use of voice-over and influenced fictional practices, I shall only touch upon a few; documentaries deserve a full-length study of their own, a study that would take full cognizance of their fluid intermixture of narration with exposition, argumentation, instruction, and poetry. Similarly, while I refer to particularly ground-breaking films by foreign directors, it was patently impossible to cover the use of narration by every national cinema. Besides, the French New Wave and Latin American (or avant-garde) filmmakers often use narration to comment upon or subvert Hollywood patterns, and my priority has been to delineate the dominant American tradition. One of the things we shall see is that although certain formats do recur, far from creating some monolithic "classic" mold, Hollywood films themselves reveal an infinite variety of uses of narration, from the staid to the downright quirky.

Before we can look at any film, however, we need a precise definition of voice-over narration. The term has often been used quite loosely; such casualness can lead to confusion and inaccuracy.

Bascially, in "voice-over narration" all three words are fully operative. *Voice* determines the medium: we must hear someone speaking. Obviously, instances of narration via printed titles or captions do not count; less obviously, one must also separate out all those cases where a text dives directly into a flashback or dream sequence without a framework of overlapping oral statements. Although voice-over narration is often used to couch flashbacks as a character's memory, the question of subjectivity in film—what Bruce Kawin calls "mindscreen"[3]—is a larger and somewhat separate issue.

Over pertains to the relationship between the source of the sound and the images on the screen: the viewer does not see the person who is speaking at the time of hearing his or her voice. Narrating asides to the camera (as in John Huston's *The Life and Times of Judge Roy Bean* [1972]), and those cases when a character does all of his or her narrating on-screen (as in Max Ophuls' *La Ronde* [1950]), certainly count as oral narration, but not as voice-*over*. "Over" actually implies more than mere screen-absence; one must distinguish voice-over from voice-*off* in terms of the space from which the voice is presumed to originate. In the latter, the speaker is merely temporarily off-camera, the camera could pan around the same scene and capture the speaker. Contrarily, voice-*over* is distinguishable by the fact that one could not display the speaker by adjusting the camera's position in the pictured story space; instead the voice comes from another time and space, the time and space of the discourse.

Narration relates to the content of the speech: someone is in the act of communicating a narrative—that is, recounting a series of events to an audience. But a difficulty appears here: in narrated films, instead of hearing a story from start to finish, we may only hear a few sentences. On the basis, sometimes, of just a fragment—a sentence or two in which, perhaps, the invisible speaker never actually recounts a past event—how does one know that the voice is *narrating* and not just conversing or thinking out loud? To put it simply, how does one know that a sentence like "I am going to go to the grocery store today even if it rains" is probably not a fragment of narration, while "It was a dark and stormy night, yet I decided to go to the grocery store" probably is?

Verb tense provides a crucial, though not conclusive, clue. In *Language in the Inner City,* the linguist William Labov notes that "narrative clauses" are clauses with a simple past tense verb (or, in some styles, a verb in the simple present). However, as Labov discovered during his research on "natural" narratives—that is, oral, unrehearsed stories recounting a personal experience—a complete narrative is made up of much more than just narrative clauses. In fact, he finds, complete narratives break down into six elements: the abstract (a short summary of the story that is about to be provided); the orientation (identification of time, place, characters, and activities); the complicating action (the unfolding of the story's events); the resolution (the climax); the evaluation (commentary elucidating the point of the story); and the coda (an epilogue, often bridging the gap between story time and the time of narrating). Thus, while the complicating action and the resolution generally use simple past tense constructions, orientations, for instance, often contain past progressive verbs.[4]

Accordingly, in considering my two little examples, we may run through a more complicated—though still instantaneous—program, testing to see whether these sentences could fit into any of the six familiar categories. "I *am going to go* to the grocery today even if it rains," with its future tense construction, may be a promise, a threat, or a bid for martyrdom, but does not immediately fulfill any of the functions that Labov details. On the other hand, "It *was* a dark and stormy night, yet I *decided to go* to the grocery store" not only contains a narrative clause, the beginning of the complicating action, but also presents a mini-orientation by describing the weather.

Mary Louise Pratt has demonstrated the general applicability of Labov's work and shown how well his six-part schema can be applied to refined, literary narratives.[5] Because voice-over narrators are often supposed to be recounting oral, unrehearsed stories of personal experience, Labov's findings are even more obviously pertinent here. Note that of the sentences quoted earlier from *Red River,* "You see, the story of the Red River D. started this way" clearly amounts to an "abstract," while the next sentence, "Along about August of 1851 . . . ," provides orientating information. With the beginning of the complicating action, the narration fades out, and the ball is passed to the images and dramatic performances. In this film the invisible speaker returns later, sometimes with evaluation, sometimes with narrative clauses, but even if he had never spoken again, we would have identified him as a narrator on the basis of the opening sentences. Regardless of how much the narrator speaks, and regardless of whether he or she ever actually recounts the action of the story, we are so familiar with the structure of narratives that the speech act as a whole is implied by the presence of any one of the six elements.

Which brings us to the point, made by Pratt through her use of speech-act theory and by Jonathan Culler in structuralist terms when he talks about a "code" of narration,[6] that as viewers, readers, listeners, and narrators, we have all not only unconsciously learned narrative structure, but also the rules and conditions *surrounding* storytelling. My grocery store examples were offered in a vacuum, yet with *Red River* a host of surrounding circumstances come into play: we already know that this is a narrative film; we match the voice's promise to tell us the story of the Red River D. with the film's title "Red River," and we recognize such genre considerations as the fact that this is a Western, Walter Brennan a common Western character actor, and his words, pronunciation, and tone appropriate for a Hollywood cowboy. In sum, one recognizes voice-over speech—fragmentary though it may be—as *narration* on the basis of: first, certain linguistic clues; secondly, our intuitive knowledge of narrative structure; and finally, the entire context in which the speech arises.

Hence, in talking about voice-over *narration,* we can and should bracket

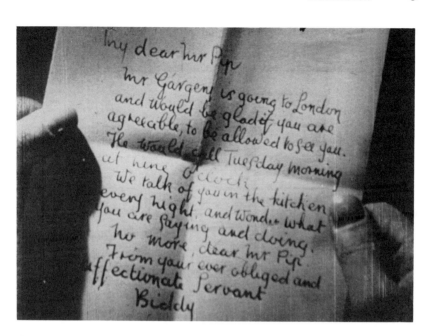

Great Expectations. Biddy [voice-over]: My dear Mr. Pip, Mr. Gargery is going to London and would be glad if you are agreeable to be allowed to see you. He would call Tuesday morning at nine o'clock. . . .

out other types of speech by invisible speakers.[7] Commercials, of course, use voice-over not to narrate, but to persuade, and school filmstrips use it to demonstrate and instruct. As for fiction films, they often use asynchronous speech to signal eavesdropping on a character's private reveries. In "interior monologue," we hear the rush of a character's thoughts or feelings in his or her own voice (Laurence Olivier uses interior monologue for Henry's soliloquies in *Henry V* [1944]); in "subjective" or "delusional" sound, we hear what the character "hears" echoing in his or her mind (frightened little Pip in David Lean's *Great Expectations* [1946] "hears" cows accusing him, "A boy with somebody else's pork pie!"). In addition, as is the case with *Great Expectations,* many films reveal the contents of a plot-turning letter or telegram by laying in the voice of author or recipient reading it out loud. On rare occasions, such as the opening of Alain Resnais's *Hiroshima mon amour* (1959), one even finds voice-over "conversations." We can separate these and other techniques from voice-over *narration* by considering their context and content.

Accordingly, "voice-over narration" can be formally defined as "oral statements, conveying any portion of a narrative, spoken by an unseen speaker situated in a space and time other than that simultaneously being presented by the images on the screen." In practice, however, one finds that distinctions blur: films may include a progressive slide from on-screen, to voice-off, to voice-over narration (e.g., *Murder, My Sweet* [Dmytryk, 1944]); interior monologue may be so interlaced with narration that the blend is undefinable (e.g., *Raw Deal* [Mann, 1948]); written titles may accompany or alternate with oral narration (e.g., *Jane Eyre* [Stevenson, 1944]), a read-aloud letter may itself relate a story (e.g., *Journey into Fear* [Foster, 1942]). I have no intention of searching for "pure" voice-over narration; so long as at some point a film does use the technique, I consider that text within this study's purview.

And then there are different types of voice-over narrators. Roughly speaking, a major division exists between "third-person," or "authorial," narrators and "first-person," or "character," narrators.* Previous critical discussions have often been skewed by treating only one of these types as representative of the technique as a whole. Worse yet, in the course of schematizing sound/image relationships, Daniel Percheron has labeled the first type "commentary" and the latter "voice-over-on-flashback." [8] His categories are inconsistent (one refers to a style of discourse prevalent in documentaries, while the other specifies a particular temporal relationship), and misleading (not all third-person narrators imitate documentaries, and not all first-person narrators recount events from their pasts). I suggest that Gérard Genette's *Narrative Discourse* [9] provides a more precise and useful method of classifying narrators. Subsequent chapters will illustrate how Genette's breakdown of narrators in terms of their narrative levels and their relationships to the stories they relate can help us separate and analyze the myriad of invisible storytellers.

"Fine. Now we understand the bounds of this study and exactly what you mean by voice-over narration. But why bother? Everyone knows that it is just a cheap shortcut, the last resort of the incompetent."

I hear this delusional voice in my mind because this attitude is extremely common both in conversation and in film literature. An examination of the ideological and theoretical underpinnings of the prejudices against the technique is the goal of chapter 1. Here let me merely admit that I have indeed seen many films with ill-conceived narration—films such as Lean's *Doctor Zhivago* (1965), where a narrator is introduced only to be ignored most of the time and then abruptly and illogically jerked in to patch up a transition; films such as Hugh Hudson's *Chariots of Fire* (1981), which set up a complicated

---

*As will be discussed in more detail in chapter 3, narrative theorists have concluded that the terms *third person* and *first person* are imprecise and misleading. However, common substitutes such as *authorial narrators* versus *character narrators* or *undramatized narrators* versus *dramatized narrators* merely foster different misconceptions. Unfortunately, the more accurate technical terms *heterodiegetic* and *homodiegetic* strike most readers as obscure or pedantic. Because *third person* and *first person* are the most common and instantly recognizable terms, I shall use them throughout this study as a shorthand method for referring to the two different relationships a narrator may have with the story he or she relates.

narrative structure that adds nothing; films such as Leslie Martinson's *P.T. 109* (1963) and Richard Benjamin's *My Favorite Year* (1982), in which the voices and their statements are pompous or banal.

However, I have seen many more films where the narration serves its purposes well and inoffensively, where it efficiently conveys important information or creates a special, intimate relationship with the viewer.

Although narration fascinates me on formal and theoretical grounds even at its clumsiest (it is precisely the defiant illogic of the narration in Otto Preminger's *Laura* [1944] that is so captivating), or even in inferior films, the technique would not have been used so often and would not be so worthy of our attention if it never soared. In scores of highly regarded films by our most competent directors the narration is so integral and adds so much that if you took it away the film would be gutted. In the course of this study I shall glance at many such films; films such as *Double Indemnity* (Wilder, 1944), *Great Expectations* (Lean, 1946), *The Lady from Shanghai* (Welles, 1948), *Letter from an Unknown Woman* (Ophuls, 1948), *Sunset Boulevard* (Wilder, 1950), *Tom Jones* (Richardson, 1963), *A Clockwork Orange* (Kubrick, 1971), *Annie Hall* (Allen, 1977), and *Days of Heaven* (Malick, 1978). I shall examine four—Ford's *How Green Was My Valley* (1941), Mankiewicz's *All About Eve* (1950), Dassin's *The Naked City* (1948), and Kubrick's *Barry Lyndon* (1975)—in close detail. My (no longer) secret agenda is for my readers to hear such films with my ears.

1

The Prejudices against Voice-Over Narration

It is past time for a reevaluation of voice-over narration. In half a century, only a few have found any kind words for the technique,[1] while scores have criticized it; no matter how many filmmakers have used it and no matter what they have actually done with it, a series of interrelated prejudices has kept us from either taking it very seriously or hearing it clearly. Upon examining these objections, however, I have discovered that both those raised many years ago and those in circulation today rest on premises that recent developments in film, narrative, and literary scholarship call into question. This chapter hopes to demonstrate that several long-cherished critical myths have clouded the subject for too long.

Images versus Words

> For sound films to be true to the basic aesthetic principle, their significant communications must originate with their pictures. . . . All the successful attempts at an integration of the spoken word have one characteristic in common: they play down dialogue with a view to reinstating the visuals.
>
> Siegfried Kracauer, *Theory of Film*

> "The question is," said Humpty Dumpty, "which is to be master—that's all."
>
> Lewis Carroll, *Through the Looking Glass*

For fifty years, a chorus of film theorists has answered "IMAGES!" As we all know, when sound was integrated with the silent film in the late 1920s, audiences were ecstatic, but certain filmmakers and almost all critics put up stiff resistance. As the years went by, the technical problems attending sound recording were swiftly remedied,[2] directors such as Mamoulian and Hitchcock began using sound creatively, and an explosion of new subject matter, styles, and characterizations made possible by dialogue hit the screen, yet the theoretical revulsion against talkies persisted. Here and there one can find a grudging acceptance of asynchronous sound or of sound effects, but the underlying tenor of the attitude towards dialogue is illustrated by Rudolf Arnheim's 1938 essay, "A New Laocoön": "Patches of speech are of little theoretical importance as long as they represent merely the minimum concession of a film director who has to meet the demands for dialogue on the part of producers and distributors. For in that case the film maker thinks of his work as a silent film, that is, as a film in the true meaning of the term, adulterated by a hostile principle."[3] More time elapsed, more technical advances were made, musicals flourished, the screwball comedies came and went, yet the critical line never swerved: if speech could not be outlawed, then it must be kept in its (lowly) place. In the past twenty years, the critical biases have softened (film historians have admitted that their predecessors went slightly overboard in outlawing dialogue); but as Rick Altman noted in 1980, "Today the primacy of the image continues to be taken as a given, even by practitioners of advanced methodologies."[4] Only in the past five years can one detect the beginnings of an unqualified acceptance of film sound and speech.

What was—or is—so very threatening about words in movies? Altman argues that the condemnation of dialogue stems from the need to divorce film from the theater, its parent and competitor, and his explanation is supported by the omnipresent expressions of fear that if speech is given free rein, film will regress to "canned theater." Advocates of a new art whose prestige was insecure were obsessed with the issue of "purity"; then and now they have sought to uncover the medium's secret, unique essence —thus the borrowing of Lessing's belief in the unique properties of each art form, and the continued search by ciné-structuralists for codes specific to the cinema. Thus, too, the chanting, over and over, like a charm to ward off evil, "Film is essentially a visual medium."

But neither the need to keep the cinema distinct from the theater, nor, more basically, the extreme anxiety over its ontology, adequately explains the near unanimity, vehemence, and persistence of the crusade to suppress film dialogue. What does "the theater" symbolize to the anti-sound critics? What else may be involved?

First, I suggest that the hatred of sound stems from dearly held notions about film's political role. Film, we read over and over again, is supposed to be the folk art, the art of the masses, the art of the immigrants, the art that would spread the Soviet revolution to the working classes of the world, or the art that will redeem the lapsed world and ennoble the common man. Yet theater has a very different reputation. As Susan Sontag has pointed out, "Theatre, by contrast [with cinema], means dressing up, pretense, lies. It smacks of aristocratic taste and class society." [5] One can practically hear Eisenstein's sneer when he predicts that talking films will imitate "highly cultured dramas." [6] Bourgeois, drawing-room plays are anathema to those who view film as an art of both broader appeal and finer sensibilities. (The same attitude can be seen today in Pauline Kael's admiration for genre films and her dislike of the pretensions of "prestige" films and adaptations.) It is rather sad and ironic, however, that for all their theoretical egalitarianism, many critics displayed elitist scorn for the movie-going public when, instead of heeding their warnings, audiences flocked to the talkies in droves.

Secondly, many critics had had special hopes for the silent cinema because of its silence. Silent film was supposed to be accessible to people of all countries; it was supposed to be the esperanto that would unite a world divided by misunderstandings and narrow nationalism, and ultimately wracked by two world wars. Although Béla Balázs would later express more acceptance of film sound than most of his colleagues, he articulated this idealism quite forcefully in 1924, when he wrote: "It will probably be the art of the film after all which may bring together the peoples and nations, make them accustomed to each other, and lead them to mutual understanding. The silent film is free of the isolating walls of language differences." [7] Speech then, is a barrier to the brave new world, a relapse into isolation and friction.

Thirdly, the anti-sound critics generally associate the drama with psychological studies of character and narrative complexity. Arnheim, for instance, contrasts what he sees as the "cinegenic species of tale," "which is full of simple happenings," and the "theater-type play" presented by the talking film, which he claims is "poor in external action but well developed psychologically." [8] Critics condemn character psychology and narrative complexity for various reasons. On the one hand, Marxist theorists wish to replace the "bourgeois fetish with individualism" with a more socially constructive emphasis on the type. On the other hand, idealistic, Romantic critics find psychological depth and elaborate narratives threatening because they had hoped that film would help integrate man with the natural world. In short, theater is used as a symbol of a kind of man-is-the-center-of-the-universe hubris, a Ptolemaic blindness that is detrimental to forging a just society or to fostering a better integration of that society with Nature.

Finally, time after time, critics claim that the theater enshrines rationality, while the silent film presents poetry. Perhaps the most astonishing attack on film dialogue is the one articulated by Kracauer in 1960: "Most important, emphasis on speech not only strengthens this tendency away from camera-life but adds something new and extremely dangerous. It opens up the region of discursive reasoning, enabling the medium to impart the turns and twists of sophisticated thought, all those rational or poetic communications which do not depend upon pictorialization to be grasped and appreciated."[9] Quite an anti-intellectual stance for so careful a scholar! And yet, perhaps, not so surprising in a century that has seen the birth of Surrealism, Dadaism, and other revolts against Victorian rationality. At any rate, something similar is echoed by other film critics. Hugo Munsterberg, for example, complains that the theater is bounded not only by space and time, but also that "whatever it shows is controlled by the same laws of causality which govern nature."[10] Silent film, on the contrary, is seen as free both of the constraints of space and time— hence open to all the montage one would wish—and of causality and rationality. In other words (sliding now from ideological to psychological speculation), theater is feared because it is seen as the realm of what Freudians call secondary process thinking—that is, conscious thought processes that recognize causality and the reality principle. Silent film, on the other hand, is seen as the realm of primary process thinking, the thinking processes of the unconscious, to which all things are possible, and/or the "magical" thought processes of young children.

In *Iconology: Image, Text, Ideology,* W. J. T. Mitchell helps us place this debate in the context of the continuing battle between those favoring images (iconophiles) and those believing that words should be master and images subservient (iconophobes). Mitchell traces this controversy from Plato through Burke and Lessing to E. M. Gombrich. He shows that many critics' prose betrays that they are judging "images" and "texts," not as neutral forms of communication, but actually as metaphors for other emotionally potent issues. Thus, images are equated with sensuality, texts with rationality; images with women, texts with men; images with the French, texts with the English and Germans. In particular Mitchell demonstrates that images have been alternately feared and venerated because of their emotive power and their connection with *graven images*—*religious icons*. Through the course of history images have, of course, had their own vehement advocates, yet the dominant tradition of Western culture has tended towards iconophobia.[11]

Thus, the stridency of the pro-image film scholars may be a defense against this dominant tradition, a quasi-conscious revolt against the traditional favoring of the abstract, intellectual word. In this revolt these critics have turned the more typical gender alignment upside down: the image is cast as the husband/father and the soundtrack as the wife/mother. The proper power relationship is made abundantly clear. As Arnheim dictates as late as 1968, "Speech, wisely subordinated, supplements, explains and deepens the image; but the image continues to rule the screen."[12] If sound takes precedence over the camera, Paul Rotha warns, it does "violence to natural instincts."[13] (Apparently, not only are natural instincts violated, but men's bodily integrity as well; Arnheim direly compares the "fruitful" man of action in the silent film with the "sterile" male characters of talkies.)

Perhaps the reason we see a flip-flop of Mitchell's paradigm in the case of film is that here we are dealing not with authoritative written texts, but with more ephemeral oral language. Indeed, instead of respecting film dialogue as a manifestation of Logos, the image-biased critics react to the soundtrack as if it were, in Christian Metz's memorable metaphor, "the chattering wife" of a great musician who must reluctantly be included in a dinner invitation to her husband.[14] Metz's "chattering wife" metaphor helps account for all those scornful expressions of disappointment at the banality of film scripts.

Obviously it is this emotional legacy of aversion to sound in general that provides the bedrock for all complaints against a particular use of the sound-track—voice-over narration. If one believes that all true film art lies in the images, then verbal narration is automatically illegitimate.*

If this ill-begotten offspring has proved too useful and popular to be out-lawed, it must, at all costs, be controlled. Thus, we can understand why even contemporary textbooks pass along the most common dictum on voice-over in film literature: "Generally, voice-over narration can be very effective *if used with restraint*" (my emphasis).[15] Furthermore, one can see this need for control as underlying the frequent, bitter accusations that ensue when uppity narration "overwhelms" or "drowns" the images.

Occasionally criticism is warranted; no one cares for a torrent of poorly scripted narration. But take the opening of Mankiewicz's *All About Eve:* here Addison DeWitt's narration literally and figuratively "overwhelms" the im-age, literally by tuning out on-screen sound and even freezing the frame, fig-uratively by providing a great deal of information with great panache. The images and dramatic action throughout this scene are more than competently handled, but clearly they support Addison's narration, not the other way around. Is the scene less interesting, less artistic, less "cinematic" because Mankiewicz has chosen to let narration play a leading role?

"Showing" versus "Telling"

> We could have had a narrator telling you what to think, that's the easy way. . . . But it's not the adult way. . . . We wanted to make the audience think and draw their own conclusion.
>
> Stanley Karnow, chief correspondent for
> "Vietnam: A Television History"

---

*This prejudice also applies to intertitles, as chapter 2 will demonstrate.

*In a movie you don't tell people things, you show
people things.*

William Goldman, *Adventures
in the Screen Trade*

According to this doctrine, when information is told to us by a narrator, it automatically becomes tainted with subjectivity—even ideological biases; only showing events without commentary allows spectators to have direct communion with the images and interpret their meaning and significance for themselves.

Such arguments correspond, as Guido Fink has also noted,[16] with the controversy in literary circles between "telling" and "showing." As we know, during the first half of this century, the followers of Henry James waged a battle against "intrusive" narrators speaking in their own voices, and in favor of the dramatization of the action in scenes devoid of overt narratorial mediation, claiming that this allows readers a closer, more objective relation to the action represented and the privilege of drawing their own interpretations. In *The Rhetoric of Fiction,*[17] Wayne Booth routed the anti-"telling" critics by questioning their presuppositions that all fiction must be "realistic," "objective," "impersonal," or "ambiguous." Moreover, we learned to see that, in literature, "showing" is just a covert form of "telling," just as removed from "reality," just as fraught with authorial manipulation. Hemingway's works, despite their avoidance of intrusive commentary by a wise narrator, are no more nor less deliberately crafted and fraught with guides to the reader's response than Thackeray's.

Granted that voice-over narration adds a certain slant, or even definite bias, to a film—why is this bad? Where are the laws saying that films have to be realistic, objective, or impersonal to begin with? Certainly no such statutes govern fiction films. However, much of the pressure against cinematic narrators comes from documentary circles in which objectivity serves as the ideal. So let us leave the subject open long enough to examine the purity of cinematic "showing."

Unlike in literature, in film the distinction between telling a story through verbal narration and showing it on the screen through images and action is not so easily discountable. These functions are carried out by quite different sign systems. On the one hand, words are arbitrary signs, the link between the signifier and the signified being merely conventional. On the other hand, semiologists who follow Charles Sanders Peirce categorize photographic images as partially "iconic" and partially "indexical" (iconic signs resemble their signifieds, indexical signs actually owe their existence to their signifieds).[18] In other words, one branch of semiotics validates the traditional, commonsense notion that images have a different, and closer, relationship to their signifieds than words. In this sense images could indeed be viewed as more "natural" or more "objective."

I am no expert on such matters, but Umberto Eco finds Peirce's notion of iconic signs illogical and untenable,[19] and Nelson Goodman sees images (even photographic images) as totally dominated by convention and hence no more "natural" than words.[20] Thus the photograph's special relationship with its signifieds is by no means incontrovertible.

Even if one were to grant that still photographs do resemble their signifieds, numerous film scholars, especially in recent years, have succeeded in depriving film of any claims to presenting nature in the raw.[21] After all, any study of individual frames reveals all sorts of meaningful manipulation—which should not be surprising, since it is precisely the job of the director, cameraman, gaffer, art director, costumer, and so on to supplement or control the meaning of each image, which is then mechanically fixed on celluloid. Furthermore, as soon as one moves from the level of the single shot to sequences of shots edited together, one moves into an area completely dependent upon cultural/ideological coding; we are now aware that both classical editing and Eisensteinian montage control the significance of the shots and the reactions of the spectators. And even before filmmakers determine how to compose or juxtapose their shots, consciously or subconsciously, they make subjective decisions regarding what to include or leave out, and these inclusions and exclusions have the force of radically altering the vision of reality presented by the film.

In film, then, while there are major differences between having the camera capture an action and having a narrator describe that action, the ideal of blissful communion between the viewer and some untouched, untainted reality presented by a completely neutral mechanism is an illusion.

But this illusion has had influential spokesmen. Look, for instance, at Roland Barthes' stand in "The Rhetoric of the Image." After a discussion of a Panzini advertisement for spaghetti products in which he himself points out the purposefulness behind the use of colors, the positioning of the products in the frame, and the studied imitation of painted still lifes, Barthes turns to describing the relationships between images and linguistic texts.

> All images are polysemous; they imply, underlying their signifiers, a "floating chain" of signifieds, the reader able to choose some and ignore others. Polysemy poses a question of meaning. . . . Hence in every society various techniques are developed intended to *fix* the floating chain of signifieds in such a way as to counter the terror of uncertain signs; the linguistic message is one of these techniques. At the level of the literal message, the text replies—in a more or less direct, more or less partial manner—to the question: *what is it?* The text helps to identify purely and simply the elements of the scene and the scene itself. . . . The denominative function corresponds exactly to an *anchorage* of all possible (denoted) meanings of the object by recourse to a nomenclature. Shown a plateful of something (in an *Amieux* advertisement), I may hesitate in

identifying the forms and masses; the caption ("rice and tuna fish with mush-rooms") helps me to choose the *correct level of perception.*

A few paragraphs later, Barthes notes that another type of relationship, which he terms "relay," is possible between linguistic texts and *moving* visual images, and here he specifically mentions film. In such cases, he admits, a linguistic text "functions not simply as elucidation but really does advance the action by setting out, in the sequences of messages, meanings that are not to be found in the image itself." We shall see later that both "anchorage" and "relay" can be quite helpful in describing the interplay between narration and images, but at this point, let us concentrate on Barthes' attitude concerning anchorage. He writes:

> When it comes to the "symbolic message," the linguistic message no longer guides identification but interpretation, constituting a kind of vice which keeps the connoted meanings from proliferating. . . . With respect to the liberty of the signifieds of the image, the text has thus a *repressive* value and we can see that it is at this level that the morality and ideology of a society are above all invested.[22]

This essay would lead one to conclude that no matter how much information has been deliberately placed within the image, it is words that anchor the viewer's identification and interpretation of the image's free and neutral signifiers, words that hold meaning in a vice, words that operate as the instruments of repression and oppression.

I believe that Barthes is telling only half the story here. Yes, the caption "rice and tuna fish with mushrooms" "anchors" meaning and resolves the ambiguity possible when looking at a collection of masses and colors. Yet, because, unlike Barthes, I do not have this advertisement in front of me, I am also aware that standing alone, "rice and tuna fish with mushrooms" is quite ambiguous. The words' connotations may tell us that this refers to a recipe or dish of some kind, but—on the level of mere identification—is it a cold salad or a hot casserole? On the level of interpretation, particularly cultural/ideological interpretation, is this a budget-saver meal (on a cheap earthenware plate set on a checked tablecloth), or a famous chef's secret concoction of wild rice and chanterelles (presented on Limoges china gleaming with subtle lighting highlights)? While the caption anchors the image, the image that Barthes has before him simultaneously anchors the meanings possible in the verbal text alone. Neither medium holds a monopoly on conveying personal, cultural, or ideological slants, and neither deserves censure for making communication possible or efficient through clearing up ambiguities.

At times filmmakers have rather blatantly used narration to alter the meaning of images. One widely reported instance involves *The North Star* (Milestone, 1943), which Lillian Hellman wrote as a piece of pro-Soviet propaganda during the wartime alliance between the United States and USSR; in the McCarthy era the film was reedited and reissued as *Armored Attack* with a narration track turning it into anti-Soviet propaganda. Yet the fact that narration (like editing) lends itself to didactic purposes has less to do with some essentially corrupting influence of words vis-à-vis images, or "telling" vis-à-vis "showing," than with the relative economy and ease of adding or altering a narration track.*

After all, images can also give powerful connotations to originally "innocent" words. Consider, for instance, the ending of Stanley Kubrick's *Dr. Strangelove* (1964) where shots of atom bombs exploding are laid over the romantic ballad "We'll Meet Again." The ballad, written by Ross Parker and Hughie Charles, and made famous by singer Vera Lynn in a 1939 recording, offers a gleam of hope on the eve of World War II. Standing alone, the song's refrain,

> We'll meet again,
> Don't know where,
> Don't know when,
> But we'll meet again
> Some sunny day,

refers to the expectations of two separating lovers to be reunited at some later date. However, in Kubrick's film the images ironically transfigure the song into a prediction that obliterated mankind will meet again in Heaven. What was bittersweet, but optimistic, becomes laughably vapid, and ultimately conveys the folly of hope.

Prejudice against voice-over for "telling" crops up over and over in remarks about narration "restricting" or "interrupting" the image track. It is easy to point to some didactic oral pronouncement, less easy to show how the editing, camera angles, or content selection have manipulated the viewer. The technique itself has become a scapegoat—often letting filmmakers who have employed it to convey offensive material off the hook.

---

*During the editing of a film, the various kinds of sound—dialogue, effects, music, room tone, narration—are kept separate from one another on perhaps dozens of distinct reels. These reels are only combined, "mixed down," to a few composite tracks towards the end of the process, and these composite tracks are ultimately used to create a final mix that is printed on the sound track of the release prints. Because the reels are kept separate for so long, adding to or altering one of the reels during post-production entails no disruption of the film's other sound elements.

"A Literary Device"

> *It is the voice-over commentary . . . a distinctly literary device.*
>
> Carolyn Lee Reitz, "The Narrative Capabilities of Prose and Film"

This ostensibly innocuous description takes us right back to the issue of purity: if voice-over is categorized as a literary technique, then by implication it is inappropriate in a pure film. But, as I am hardly the first to notice, the question of purity is a fake issue: film is a young art form, and it has borrowed photography, dance, music, costume design, storylines, even the quintessentially "cinematic" concept of montage, from numerous and sundry sources. The history of film is the history of assimilating and reinterpreting techniques and materials from other art forms. Even if voice-over were a literary device, it would be no less valuable, no less valid a technique than any other that film has retailored to serve its own purposes.

However, although literature has undeniably been a major influence on voice-over narration, I am not willing to concede that such narration is a "distinctly literary device" in the first place. This label depends upon two dubious assumptions concerning the interrelation of narrative, literature, and film. For one thing, it implies that narration is a subset of literature—yet narrative is the larger kingdom, narrative literature only a phylum, and novels and short stories only species. Moreover, it implies that narration is intrinsically foreign to film. Yet Scholes and Kellogg demonstrate in *The Nature of Narrative*[23] (and their argument has been widely seconded)[24] that film is more accurately assigned to narrative than to drama. For myself, try as I might, I cannot place film wholly under narrative's umbrella. There seems to me a core component, the quasi-presence of the actors and their independent contributions to the text, that links the medium with drama. However, at any rate, adding oral narration to a film does not interject a literary technique into an unadulterated dramatic form (once again, it does not introduce "telling" to an untainted "show"), all it does is superimpose another type of narration on top of a mode that is already at least partly narrative.

Aside from the issue of purity, shackling voice-over to literature leads to false expectations. Brain Henderson argues that voice-over narrators fail to replicate the functions of novel narrators: cinematic narrators are not consistently present; they are not as well integrated with the rest of the narrative discourse; they do not necessarily color the text by their point of view; in short, he concludes, "They are ludicrous stand-ins for the novelistic 'I'."[25] Yet Henderson's angry tone seems misplaced once we drop the false analogy between voice-over and literary narration. Actually, if one *had* to choose a formal analogue for the voice-over narrator, I suggest one would do better to look in the opposite direction—that is, at the use of narrators in the theater.

Since we think of the theater as the domain of drama, we may forget how often and how persistently the stage has chosen to incorporate narration. The Greeks and Romans, of course, used choruses; the medieval miracle plays included prologues; many forms of oriental theater have traditionally used narration alongside dramatic action. Closer to home in the English theater, Shakespeare used narration in *Henry V, Romeo and Juliet,* and *Troilus and Cressida,* Marlowe in *Dr. Faustus;* witty prologues and epilogues were de rigueur during the Restoration, and only slightly less common throughout the eighteenth century. Although narration was avoided during the heyday of dramatic realism, in our own century theatrical narration has been employed by, among others, Bertolt Brecht, Thornton Wilder, Tennessee Williams, and Arthur Miller.

Theatrical narrators often differ from voice-over narrators in some respects: they generally stand in sight on stage rather than wafting in as disembodied voices; choruses serve more as surrogates for the audience than as substitutes for an author; prologues and epilogues only bracket the story proper with abstracts, orientations, and codas, and do not directly narrate the action. Yet even these differences can sometimes be similarities: in some films narrators do appear on screen, and in scores narration is used merely as prologue or epilogue. Furthermore, the intrinsic connections between the two types of narrators are striking. Because theatrical narration, like voice-over, is first, intermittent; secondly, interwoven with dramatic scenes that are not mediated through that narrator; and thirdly—crucially—*spoken aloud,* it parallels voice-over narration's formal characteristics much more closely than novel narration.

One might think that Henderson's criticisms would at least be relevant for adaptations, films that do present voice-over narrators as if they were the narrators of novels. But I do not believe that his exposé has much force—of course these narrators are shams. In these adaptations the filmmakers are indeed using the narrators as stand-ins for the novels' narrators, just as in *Red River* Hawks would like us to believe that the unseen voice is a Western tale teller, just as in *To Be or Not to Be* (1942) Ernst Lubitsch pretends that his narrator is a radio newscaster. "Novel narrator" is a particularly common pose, but hardly the only one.

Discussions such as Henderson's imply that such posing is a trick, as if Hollywood were conspiratorially trying to pass off false goods. However, if one objects to the poses that voice-over narrators assume or if one stringently expects them to fulfill all the functions of their models, then logically one should also object to hundreds of novels, plays, poems, and films that employ similar pretenses. Texts from one medium or genre commonly borrow the trappings of another—novels pretend to be diaries, letters, oral tales; plays pretend to be newspapers, chronicles, dreams; poems pretend to be images, plays, or monologues. We never berate Conrad's storytellers for speaking too long and with too much polish for a real oral storyteller; we rarely take Richardson's epistolary narrators to task for their preposterous letters; we don't criticize Browning's monologuists because they lack the gestures, costumes, and makeup of an actor on the stage. Pip's intermittent voice-over in Lean's *Great Expectations* is in no way equivalent to Pip's continuous narration in the novel, but the former brings the latter to mind and serves some of the same purposes. Why should this practice be seen as "ludicrous"?

Like other art forms, narrated films resort to all sorts of castles in the air, all sorts of masquerades. Identifying and examining these masquerades is important; but just because many voice-over narrators masquerade as novel narrators does not mean that the device itself is *essentially* literary.

"Redundancy"

> *Most documentary theorists are agreed that the one cardinal rule in the use of [voice-over] is to avoid duplicating the information in the image. The commentary should provide only what's not apparent on the screen.*
>
> Louis Giannetti, *Understanding Movies*

A fourth critical myth related to the preceding ones, the argument for shunning "redundancy," can be traced back to the late 1920s, when one group of theorists figured out a way to incorporate sound that would minimize its pull towards synchronous dialogue. In 1928 the famous Soviet "Statement on the Sound Film" argued against sound that adhered to or accompanied the image (which, they claimed, would restrict montage) and advocated nonsynchronous, contrapuntal sound.[26] However little this theory has held sway in practice, it has been extremely influential in critical discussions: René Clair and Paul Rotha repeated it, and film history textbooks trace the maturing of the integration of sound on the basis of how much directors have divorced the sound track from the image.

Since by definition voice-over involves the separation of the picture of the narrator and the sound of his or her voice, in some respects the contrapuntal theory actually favors this technique. However, the theory became a double-edged sword: it has led to the banning of any narration that corresponds closely with the images on the screen. Contemporary textbooks pass on criticisms of redundancy: in *Elements of Film*, Lee Bobker refers to it as "double-telling" and claims that it "represents the worst possible use of narration."[27]

This prejudice displays a certain insensitivity to the kinds of information provided via words and via the scenic presentation. The image of an object

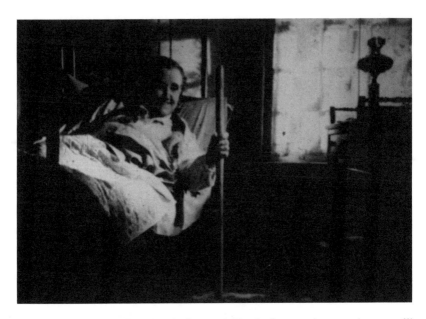

How Green Was My Valley. Huw [voice-over]: For the first month my mother was still upstairs and we would talk to each other with tappings.

and the verbal description of that object exist on two different planes. Strictly speaking, "double-telling" is impossible: different information will always be provided by different sign systems. The most that can be said is that in some instances (and these are rather rare in fiction films), the viewer notes a certain overlap between the information provided visually and that provided by the narration.

Is such overlapping always a flaw? In *The Old Man and the Sea* (John Sturges, 1958), we see a close-up of the old man (Spencer Tracy) opening his eyes, looking bewildered, and slowly smiling, while off-screen the narrator says, "The old man opened his eyes and for a long moment he was coming back from a long way away. Then he smiled." One can distinguish a gap here between the verbalization of the action—with the specific details about the old man being a "long way away"—and the visualization of that action—complete with the exact nuances of the old man's expression and the warm colors of his sun-beaten face. Yet, in either medium, the action seems banal, the emphasis on it inexplicable, and the overlap works against the simplicity and spareness of Hemingway's style. On the other hand, *How Green Was My Valley* contains many instances of overlapping images and narration; we both witness and hear about Huw and his bedridden mother communicating by tapping on the floor, we both witness and hear about the distribution of the spending

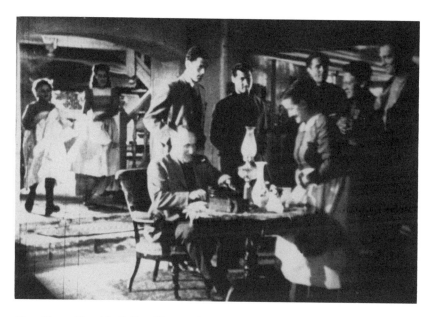

How Green Was My Valley. Huw [voice-over]: After dinner when dishes had been washed, the box was brought to the table for the spending money to be handed out.

money. This overlapping relates to the cherishing of these moments by the older, nostalgic narrator—we linger over these moments contentedly, sharing the double perspective of the reflecting narrating-I and the participating child. This lingering forces the spectator to view such simple familial details as emblematic of all that is lost; as Guido Fink remarks, "Things must be twice-told in order to be safely redeemed from time and decay." [28] Far from being an egregious fault, this overlap is a modest plum.

"The Last Resort of the Incompetent"

> *Is it [voice-over narration] a meaningful conven-*
> *tion . . . Or is it an emergency cord the filmmaker*
> *pulls when he or she cannot think of another way*
> *to begin a movie or deliver some important piece of*
> *information?*
>
> Bernard Dick, *Anatomy of Film*

According to another common view, since real filmmakers know that film is essentially a visual medium, it is the unimaginative and incompetent who turn to voice-over. Ironically, along with the fundamental anti-sound bias, voice-over narration's reputation has suffered from the advantages it offers, such as its facility in conveying expositional information.

Furthermore, because recording synchronous sound on location is some-times impossible and always time-consuming, and thus expensive, taping voice-over narration in a controlled studio setting is comparatively simple and economical. The technique is so much easier that it is highly recommended for home movies—"Say It with Narration" counsels *Super-8 Filmmaker*,[29] and *Movie Maker* labels it "The Technique Amateurs Should Make Their Own."[30] Guilty by association, the technique now carries an aura of penny-pinching and unprofessionalism.

And yet . . . are there aesthetic merit points for doing things the hard way? If using voice-over allows one to include important exteriors, as it does in *The Naked City*'s use of scenes shot on the noisy streets of New York, so much the better.

Another advantage voice-over offers is its ability to rectify mistakes. Even in big-budget features, because it is added during post-production, when the filmmakers may have identified any troubles with the rough cut's continuity, intelligibility, or tone, voice-over can be used as last-minute patchwork. Lillian Ross reveals that when John Huston's *The Red Badge of Courage* (1951) was shown in preview, the audience responded by laughing at what were supposed to be the most tragic moments. Panic-stricken, the producers decided that the way to instill proper respect for the text was to add voice-over: in the final version, the film opens with an authoritative voice (James Whit-more), giving a mini-lecture about Crane and the novel's themes; Whitmore also narrates the body of the text with quotations from the novel.[31] Similarly, the narration in *Red River* was a late addition: in previews the film appeared to be overlong, so transitions that had originally been accomplished via lengthy shots of handwritten pages of "Early Tales of Texas" were replaced with Brennan's voice-over.

In both cases, production histories expose narration as a last-minute conve-nience. But what matters is not whether the narration was a forethought or an afterthought, but how well it is thought out. The opening of *The Red Badge of Courage* is heavy-handed and schoolmarmish. Yet in *Red River*, the voice-over not only streamlines the film, but also makes it more intimate and con-versational, and less pretentiously pseudo-legendary.[32]

I do not believe in prescriptive criticism under any flag, whether onto-logical or ideological. Ultimately our assessment of the merits of a film's nar-ration (and other issues of film form) should depend upon the case, not on a priori legislation.

2

Ancestors, Influences, and Development

In chapter 1, I questioned the conventional notion that films caught voice-over (like the measles?) from novels; it thus behooves me to present an alternate and more detailed account of the technique's development. Tracing the birth and history of a cinematic technique is a risky business; without having seen *every* film made since 1927, I cannot be sure that the trends I perceive from my research on several hundred are accurate for the thousands that have been produced. What follows is necessarily offered only as a working hypothesis.

Such hypothesizing is worthwhile, however, because only by sketching in a macrocosmic model can we see how a technique such as voice-over narration becomes part of the cinema's repertoire, where it came from, when and why its role ebbed or grew, who used it and in what kinds of films. And the answers to such questions provide crucial grounding for aesthetic issues (such as, how does narration really work in a film? what kinds of effects does it have?) addressed in subsequent chapters.

Lecturers and Intertitles in the Silent Era

In a sense, movies started with voice-over narration. During the medium's very beginnings in the late 1890s, when films consisted of just one unbroken take, and programs were structured by stringing several of these little films together, exhibitors often employed "lecturers" to provide running commentaries for the audience.

The history of the use of these lecturers has been traced by Charles Musser and Charles Berg.[1] At the turn of the century, as films grew longer and more complex, the need for and use of lecturers grew rather than declined; for instance, lecturers were a standard component of novelty traveling exhibitions such as the popular Hale's Tours (1905–). As for early fiction films, their storylines were often inaccessible to audiences both because of viewers' inexperience at "reading" narrative images, and because of the filmmakers' lack of skill in conveying temporal, spatial, and narrative relationships, thus lecturers could potentially fill a crucial gap. Some major production companies issued lecture notes along with each of their films, and film critics, such as W. Stephen Bush of *The Moving Picture World*, actively campaigned for more oral guidance.

Lecturers reached their peak of popularity in the United States in the early 1910s. Even in their heyday many exhibitors did without; qualified lecturers were hard to find and cost money, and since they didn't always get a chance to view the films before they were shown (the programs changed so frequently), their commentaries were not always well prepared or helpful. Their decline was precipitated by the fact that by 1912 filmmakers had developed editing and narrative strategies that made visual storytelling more sophisticated and comprehensible (needing less explanation), and these innovations led directly to longer films (more taxing to narrate orally). Moreover, as Charles Berg points out, the subsequent move to larger picture palaces precipitated the decline of lecturers because of the difficulties of voice projection in such large spaces. Finally, the industry turned to more standardization of product and consolidation of editorial control in the hands of film producers, not individual exhibitors. By including intertitles in their films, producers could ensure that no matter where the film was exhibited, or under what conditions, every audience would receive the necessary narrative information.

Intriguingly, in Japan, where various forms of drama such as Kabuki and doll plays had traditionally separated dramatic action and narrative information, the marriage of human storytellers and silent films lasted for two more decades. Lecturers, or *benshi*s, were a customary part of performances until 1937. The *benshi*s wielded great power (for example, they had the authority to insist on changes in a print that displeased them), and they effectively delayed the coming of sound in Japanese cinema for years. Their power grew out of their popularity: many spectators would visit theaters not so much to see the film as to see and hear their favorite *benshi* narrate, and they would greet him by enthusiastically calling out his nickname. Although in the United States lecturers seem to have been employed primarily for clarity and convenience, the fact that Japanese lecturers were more popular with audiences than movie stars demonstrates the affective potential of filmic narration.[2]

Intertitles (alternatively called "subtitles") also count as an ancestor of voice-over narration, and they too started with the birth of the cinema. During the industry's infancy such titles were added by exhibitors, who placed them on lantern slides, but from at least 1903 on producers frequently included intertitles in their reels. Once again, film reviews of the time testify to the need: *The Dramatic Mirror,* for instance, objected to one film because "it is not as clearly told in the pictures as we would like to see. . . . The Edison company would do well producing complicated dramatic stories of this kind if it would insert descriptive paragraphs at the proper points in the films so the spectators might gain a knowledge of what the actors are about." [3]

However, titles were not only a means of conveying expository information. The earliest titles were generally spare, merely identifying or temporal indicators presented on plain backgrounds in undistinguished typeface, but as the silent era progressed, and intertitles won out over lecturers as the principal source of narration, filmmakers began to pay more attention to their titling. D. W. Griffith, for one, exploited intertitles effectively early on; William K. Everson reminds us that the titles of *Intolerance* (1916) skillfully link stories of four different centuries, using different lettering and graphic backgrounds for each. [4] Moreover, Griffith habitually took advantage of his titles to judge his characters, make personal asides, or draw parallels between the screen action and current events—in short, to open up a direct line of communication between himself and his audience and to suggest a personal tone of voice. *Way Down East* (1920), for example, begins with titles enforcing Griffith's moral: "Once man had been polygamous. . . . [but] The truth must bloom that his [man's] happiness lies in his purity and constancy. . . . If there is anything in this story that brings home to man the suffering caused by our selfishness, perhaps it will not be in vain." Griffith's narrating "voice" is unappealing to modern tastes (too florid and preachy), but consider how clearly we hear it, and how much it colors our experience of his works.

In the late teens and twenties, title writing became an art in itself. Sometimes overzealousness led to ghastly purplish prose, but the writers often succeeded in creating a legendary atmosphere for Westerns and epics or in adding a witty perspective to comedies. And filmmakers constantly experimented with changes in typeface and graphics, or, as was the case with Soviet filmmakers, with rhythmically integrating the written text into their montage.

Intriguingly, critical attitudes to intertitles anticipate the prejudices against voice-over narration. As mentioned above, reviewers initially clamored for more titles, and the technique has always had advocates. (Iris Barry once wrote: "In employing a chorus . . . to bridge space and time the Greek and the Japanese dramatists alike found a valuable convention. And the sub-title is really to the film what the chorus was to those dramas.") [5] Yet in the later silent era the pendulum swung in the other direction. Critical wisdom decreed that "The fewer words printed on the screen the better. . . . The ideal film has no words printed on it at all, but is one unbroken sheet of photography." [6] At the very end of the silent era, film grammar and audience familiarity with that grammar had developed to the point where a film as satisfying as F. W. Murnau's *The Last Laugh* (1924) could eschew titles, but this was a late and rare development.[7]

Thus, far from verbal narration being a belated and supplemental addition to the cinema, from film's earliest days it was regularly interleaved with dramatic action. Such narration was necessary for clarity, but it also expanded the types of material a film could convey, and individualized and personalized the telling of the story. Evidence of its value can be drawn from the fact that titling has persisted into sound films; it was especially common in the 1930s and 1940s, and still figures prominently in current releases. And lecturing has been transfigured and reborn in the sound era by a technique that has solved all the earlier problems with preparation, audibility, and standardization—voice-over narration.

Radio

Lecturers and intertitles are voice-over narration's direct kin, but it owes at least as much, if not more, to a collateral relative: radio.

In line with film scholarship's image bias, the compelling connections between radio and cinema have been generally ignored. The two media are closely intertwined: both profited from the same technical innovations, such as Lee De Forest's audion tube for sound amplification, with formal radio broadcasting (1920) preceding the talkies (1926–27) by just a few years. Early radio stations were sometimes acquired by the owners of local motion picture theaters, and corporate links connected CBS with Paramount and RCA with RKO. In the 1930s, along with technical and corporate entanglements, the two media shared stars and stories. Several radio series, such as "Lux Radio Theater," which was hosted by Cecil B. De Mille, presented adaptations of current hit pictures with film stars recreating their roles, while the film studios, on the other hand, both produced films such as *The Big Broadcast* series, which revolved around radio formats, and enticed major radio stars (such as Bob Hope and Bing Crosby) into features. Directors, producers, and screenwriters who originally worked in radio include Jules Dassin, John Houseman, Howard Koch, Arch Oboler, Abraham Polonsky, Irving Reis, and Orson Welles.

Given this close relationship, the development of narration in radio is extremely pertinent. During the middle 1920s radio stations primarily broadcast music recitals and sports events; it was not until later in the decade that radio began regularly to offer serials and other shows with fictional storylines. Although announcers and hosts were part of radio from its very inception, some early dramatic shows avoided narration and "imitated the all-dialogue drama of the theater."[8] A program such as "First Nighter," which began in 1929, "simulated a theater atmosphere. The dramas were billed as being broadcast from 'The Little Theater off Times Square' . . . Mr. First Nighter was always shown to his seat by an 'usher' just before curtain time. . . . After the commercial a buzzer would sound and the usher would call out 'Curtain going up!'"[9] But narration soon triumphed: in "Death Valley Days" (1930–45) the Old Ranger figured as storyteller, and "The Lone Ranger" (1933–54) used an anonymous voice who kept track of what was happening meanwhile back at the ranch. Throughout the 1930s (and into the 1940s) narration appealed to the most creative radio playwrights. Norman Corwin singles out the present-tense immediacy of the narration in Archibald MacLeish's "The Fall of the City," the use of multiple narrators in Stephen Vincent Benét's "John Brown's Body" and the intricate chronology of his own "They Fly through the Air."[10] Erik Barnouw cites the use of proxy listeners (i.e., "narratees") in "Death Valley Days," stream-of-consciousness in Arch Oboler's horror series "Lights Out," and the "footnote narration" in Corwin's charming "The Plot to Overthrow Christmas."[11]

Corwin, Oboler, and MacLeish all won fame for their innovative scripts and for their narration in particular, but for our purposes, the most important figure in radio narration was Orson Welles. Welles was immersed in radio; in the mid thirties he had read for "The March of Time," "The Shadow," and other popular shows, and from July 1938, when he and Houseman created "The Mercury Theater of the Air," to March 1940, he adapted, narrated, and acted in nearly eighty radio plays.[12] Welles's contribution was to turn radio stories towards narrative and decisively away from pure drama. As James Naremore states:

> Welles always thought of radio . . . as a narrative medium rather than a purely dramatic one. . . . Welles wanted to eliminate the "impersonal" quality of such [pseudo-theatrical] programs, which treated the listener like an eavesdropper. . . . The Mercury program would therefore be called "First Person Singular" . . . and all its broadcasts, from *A Tale of Two Cities* to *Hamlet* would be done in first-person narrative, together with related devices such as stream of consciousness, diaries and letters.[13]

"The Mercury Theater of the Air" produced not only the infamous "The War of the Worlds," but also adaptations of *Heart of Darkness, Jane Eyre, Dracula, The Magnificent Ambersons, Sherlock Holmes,* and *Treasure Island.*

Critics reacted favorably to Welles's program,* but overall opinion regarding narration oscillated between suspicious disapproval and enthusiastic adherence, prompting one wag to ask, "Is narration being worn long or short

---

*See, for instance, the *New York Times* review on 24 July 1938: "The 'first-person' [technique] makes his [Welles's] role more personal than the standard radio narrator; he becomes part of the tale and it moves more smoothly and naturally than it might under the ordinary, rapid-fire announcerial style" (sec. 9, p. 10).

this year?" [14] Max Wylie, director of continuity at CBS, articulated the major complaint when he stated: "In a dramatic broadcast, any narration amounts to an interruption. Continuity of illusion has been dislocated. We have been taken out of our play. . . . And because I know of no broadcast play which was left undamaged by this device, I consider it risky and inadvisable." [15] On the other hand, Archibald MacLeish wrote in a foreword to "The Fall of the City": "The Announcer is the most useful dramatic personage since the Greek Chorus. . . . His presence is as natural as it is familiar. And his presence . . . restores to the poet that obliquity, that perspective, that three-dimensional depth without which great poetic drama cannot exist." [16] Again we see the tussle between "showing" and "telling," between "transparency" and "intrusiveness," and the linkage of narration not to literature but to the theater.

The direct influence of radio narration on certain films will be apparent as we proceed. In general, radio provided filmmakers with examples of all flavors of oral narration—folksy, authoritative, poetic, and bland—and of complicated narrative structures. It also showed film how to bring a novel's narrative voice to life, rather than simply mining the text for plot and characters. Moreover, given the fact that lecturers, intertitles, and documentary commentators practically always narrated in the third person, other than novels themselves, radio was the cinema's major role-model for first-person narration. Finally, as anyone who has ever heard thirties radio drama can testify, radio simply illustrated to one and all the spellbinding power of the human voice.

Newsreels, Short Subjects, and Documentaries

Before narration was common in fiction films, it went through an apprenticeship in newsreels, shorts, and documentaries. The limitations of early sound-recording equipment—sound cameras and optical recording devices were enormously heavy and bulky, and microphones nonselective, amplifying background noises as much as the desired audio source—encouraged this turn to narration, since if a filmmaker wanted to take his cameras out of doors, away from the insular and insulated sound studios, his best bet was to shoot the exteriors silent, and add narration, effects, and music later. Certainly shooting silently and adding narration was the cheapest method of production, and these films have always had to cope with low budgets. But convenience and economy were not the only reasons why these films turned to voice-over: narration provided the perfect means of conveying all the discursive and expository information relevant to nonfiction subject matter, of linking materials from various times and locales, and of amalgamating archival, stock, reenactments, graphics, and location footage.

Radio provided the catalyst. The first sound newsreels were released in 1927; they recorded events in synchronous sound and provided explanations and transitions by means of intertitles. But in January 1930, Universal took out a full page ad in *Variety* addressed to theater exhibitors: "Now you can present the world's most famous radio broadcaster as the Talking Reporter in Universal Newsreel. . . . Now you can have an attraction in your newsreel never before equalled." [17] Shrewdly recognizing the potential advantages of this device, *Variety*'s reviewer wrote: "With its silent newsreel and Graham McNamee giving it sound through speech, Universal appears to have something worth while as a newsreel and a comedy possibility." [18] Needless to say, the competing newsreels adopted narration immediately.

And then there was *The March of Time*. This series started in 1931 as a radio program with dialogue vignettes recreating news events strung together by authoritative narration. In 1935 the program was reborn as a quasi-newsreel produced by Louis de Rochemont, who had previously been head of short subjects for Fox Movietone Corp. *The March of Time* differed from all other newsreels—it was longer, it gave more focused attention to its topics, it was released less frequently, it used more reenactments, and it was both more partisan and more controversial. [19] But perhaps the most distinctive feature of the series was the authoritative, booming narrator making grand statements about world events. Officially, this narrator, Westbrook Van Voorhis, was referred to as "The Voice of Time," but he came to be known as "The Voice of God."

The March of Time was immensely popular and influential, winning a special Academy Award in 1937, reaching its zenith preceding and during World War II. As John Grierson once noted, "In a world which is sure of nothing, it [the voice] is supremely sure of itself." [20] The style of *The March of Time*'s narration was so distinctive and so effective that in many people's minds it is still synonymous with cinematic narration.

Other short-subject films of the thirties made narration an integral part of their modus operandi. Travelogues and educational films used it straightforwardly, but often lighthearted pieces, such as *Pete Smith's Specialties*, exploited the comic possibilities *Variety* had presciently recognized the moment narration came on the scene. Furthermore, from the very beginning of the 1930s, humorous and/or inappropriate narration was frequently laid over compilations of archival footage, providing a cheap means of recycling resources. (This principle lies behind a 1940s series called *Flicker Flashbacks*, which wedded clips from silent films with incongruous narration and titles.) And previews of coming attractions have consistently turned to narration as the best method of persuading the audience to come back next week.

As for documentaries proper, during the early 1930s the creative center was the group gathered in London around John Grierson, producing films first for the Empire Marketing Board and later for the General Post Office. This group not only used narration liberally, but experimented with it, extending its possibilities. *The Song of Ceylon* (Wright, 1934) drew part of its commentary from the journal of a seventeenth-century traveler to Ceylon; *Housing Problems* (Anstey and Elton, 1935) had the subjects of the film narrate their own stories straight to the camera; and *Coalface* (Cavalcanti, 1936) dabbled with verse narration. But perhaps the most successful of their experiments was *Night Mail* (Watt, 1936) which simply traces the journey of the night mail train from London to Aberdeen. With a score by Benjamin Britten and narration written by W. H. Auden that is meshed to the pace of the train, Watt made the simple story into something magical. Over shots of the train speeding through empty countryside we hear:

> Pulling up feet at a steady climb,
> The gradient's against her but she's on time.
> Past cotton grass and moor and boulder,
> Shoveling white steam over her shoulder,
> Snorting noisily as she passes
> Silent miles of wind-swept grasses.

Perhaps not Auden's best poetry, but it serves to capture and ennoble this facet of everyday life.

Narrated documentaries were produced in the United States during the early thirties, but for our purposes, the most important releases appeared later in the decade, when Pare Lorentz directed *The Plow That Broke the Plains* (1936) and *The River* (1937) for the U.S. Resettlement Administration. The first presented the history of the despoiling of the Great Plains, the second, the story of the Mississippi River. Both films blended musical scores by Virgil Thomson with lyrical narration spoken by operatic baritone Thomas Chalmers. The voice-over in *The River,* with its lists and lists of names of rivers, drew comparisons to Whitman's poetic catalogues, and was greatly applauded. Most important, unlike the British classics and other noteworthy documentaries made abroad, through critical acclaim and shrewd publicity, both of Lorentz's films triumphed over initial distribution problems and reached the general American public. *The Plow That Broke the Plains* played a circuit of independent theaters, and *The River,* distributed by Paramount and "seen by millions of people in more than 5000 theaters . . . at last made the word 'documentary' a part of the vocabulary of the nation." [21] In so doing, they began to familiarize the American public with documentary-style narration.

Lorentz's breakthroughs notwithstanding, up until World War II Hollywood had held itself aloof from documentaries both because it wished to avoid controversial social and political issues, and because it was locked into its studio-based production practices. But when documentaries were assigned crucial wartime tasks—educating the public as to the reasons behind the conflict, keeping up morale, teaching the troops military procedures—the Dream Factory could keep aloof no longer. Studios were hired to produce certain documentaries, and when the government opened up or expanded its own film units, it recruited or conscripted numerous Hollywood professionals, including Frank Capra, Philip Dunne, John Ford, Carl Foreman, John Huston, Walter Huston, Anatole Litvak, Alfred Newman, Louis de Rochemont, Dimitri Tiomkin, and Malvin Wald. Wartime documentaries employed various styles of narration: the British *A Diary for Timothy* (Jennings, 1945) is a lyrical memoir of the war at home addressed to a newborn infant; *The True Glory* (Reed and Kanin, 1945), a British-American co-production, merges an anonymous, authoritative narrator and voices purporting to belong to General Eisenhower and dozens of common soldiers. But usually wartime documentaries, such as the widely seen and greatly influential *Why We Fight* series produced by Capra and Litvak, needed to convey a great deal of information with complete conviction. Thus instead of using Lorentz or the Grierson school as a model, their narration is very much in the mold of *The March of Time*—loud, authoritative, exhortative.

Fiction Films, 1930–1950

Evidence suggests that the earliest experiments with narration in fictional contexts were made overseas: in 1930 Cocteau spoke a voice-over commentary for his *Le Sang d'un poète,* and in *M* (1931) Fritz Lang placed the police commissioner's telephone conversations explaining his efforts to track down the child-murderer over shots of the detectives following up clues. As for English-language cinema, William Everson has brought to my attention a (quite forgettable) film entitled *Forgotten Commandments,* directed by Gasnier and Schorr in 1932. This film, like shorts of the time, uses narration for recycling: a priest tells a group of children the story of Moses in voice-over while the screen shows scenes from *The Ten Commandments,* Cecile B. De Mille's 1923 silent extravaganza.

Yet owing to fossilized remnants of a vigorous publicity campaign, it is easy to pinpoint the earliest extensive use of narration in American fiction film: *The Power and the Glory,* directed by William K. Howard, written by Preston Sturges in 1933. The film starts with Henry, Tom Garner's lifelong best friend, returning from Garner's funeral. That night, in order to counter his wife's criticism of the deceased, Henry tells her the story of Garner's life over a series of achronological flashbacks. This story concerns the rise and fall of a powerful man: Garner started poor and uneducated, but through the aid of his first wife became a railroad magnate, only to lose his business, cause his first wife's death, learn that his son and mistress/second wife have cheated on him, and commit suicide. Henry narrates extensively, bridging ellipses, commenting on events, even speaking the other characters' dialogue for them during an exterior scene. Sturges wrote to his father, "It is neither a silent film nor a talking film, but rather a combination. It embodies the action of a silent picture, the reality of voice and the storytelling economy and richness of characterization of a novel." [22] The publicity people at Twentieth-Century Fox labeled Sturges's technique "narratage," but it is never clear exactly which technique(s) "narratage" refers to—the structuring of the story out of achronological flashbacks, the use of voice-over, the narrator speaking the characters' dialogue, or some combination. Nonetheless, the film's originality was widely heralded: "The ballyhoo included putting a bronze tablet in the New York theater where it opened to commemorate 'the first motion picture in which narratage was used as a method of telling a dramatic story.' " [23]

Unfortunately, the negative of *The Power and the Glory* was destroyed in a fire, and all we now have to go on are reconstructions. The print I saw is disjointed and singularly uninspiring, which helps explain why, despite all the publicity, the film was a commercial flop. Moreover, the narration itself is not particularly impressive. One reviewer, Richard Watts, Jr., astutely notes that Henry is a colorless cipher and his storytelling quite bland; unlike, say, Fitzgerald's *The Great Gatsby,* the manner of telling the tale does not provide valuable insights into the narrator's personality or into his relationship with the protagonist.* This intricate use of voice-over seems to have sprung fully formed from Sturges's brow, but the babe was stillborn.

Nevertheless, one can hardly overestimate the importance of *The Power and the Glory* in the history of cinematic narration. Screenwriters saw and admired it (Philip Dunne has recognized that it was a major influence on his scripting of *How Green Was My Valley*),[24] and the parallels between it and *Citizen Kane* are compelling (though denied by Welles). But the pathbreaker's effect was far from immediate. Although in the years that followed, other films incorporated narration (James Whale's *The Bride of Frankenstein* [1935] uses it to recycle footage from the original *Frankenstein*), voice-over did not become common in America until 1939. This cannot be explained by technological limitations, because Hollywood films of the thirties were quite able to employ sophisticated sound editing and rerecording.[25] Why then? What factors kept it from being used throughout the 1930s, and why did the situation change at the end of the decade?

To begin with, when sound was originally developed, Hollywood turned to the closest role model it could find—the theater. Dialogue coaches, stage actors and actresses, and stage directors were imported wholesale to California, and the first decade of sound was filled with adaptations of (non-narrated) plays such as *Anna Christie, Ah! Wilderness,* and *Private Lives.* Although one could also point to numerous adaptations of novels, with the studios so

---

*Watt's comments about "narratage" are equally revealing: "This mysterious new method of cinema storytelling . . . turned out last night to be little more than the famous old invention of the cut-back, combined with one of the important functions of the *radio announcer*" (*New York Herald Tribune,* 17 Aug. 1933, sec. 1, p. 12; my emphasis).

oriented towards the theater and towards song and dance, the novels' narrative voices were either ignored or relegated to intertitles.

Also, when sound was a new phenomenon, audiences apparently were fascinated by synchronicity per se. Lewis Jacobs believes that they would have felt cheated if speech had not come from the lips of the actors; thus Mary Ann Doane argues that voice-off and voice-over could only be incorporated once the novelty of synchronous speech had worn off.[26]

The situation changed in 1939 owing to the convergence of several factors. First and foremost, as I mentioned earlier, it was in the late 1930s that radio narration came into its fullest flower, with among other noteworthy programs, the Mercury Theater's literary adaptations. Orson Welles's move to Hollywood in 1939 is symbolic of the migration of the device from one medium to the other. The influence of Welles's radio experience on his own subsequent film career is marked· in all, two-thirds of Welles's finished feature films use voice-over. While other directors have also repeatedly favored narration, no one else has used it so much or so creatively. When we consider that along with continuing his connection with radio drama down through the years, Welles has also habitually read the narration tracks of other people's films (from Edward Ludwig's *Swiss Family Robinson* [1940] to Mel Brooks's *History of the World, Part I* [1981]), we see clearly the imprint that radio narration made on Welles, and the influence that his delight in narration has had on the history of American cinema. Arthur Knight's mistaken assertion that voice-over narration in fiction films began with *Citizen Kane* (1941) and *The Magnificent Ambersons* (1942)[27] is both understandable and telling; no one else has so closely associated his work—and his own voice—with narration as Welles.

Secondly, as I have taken pains to show above, it was at exactly this moment that classic documentaries such as *The Plow That Broke the Plains, The River,* and Willard Van Dyke and Ralph Steiner's *The City* (the hit of the 1939 World's Fair) first reached a wide American audience. It was also in 1939 that the start of World War II in Europe gave newsreels topics of great moment to report to news-hungry audiences.

In 1939 several major releases incorporating voice-over, including *Wuthering Heights, Juarez, The Roaring Twenties,* and *Confessions of a Nazi Spy,* simultaneously appeared, and the ice was broken. At the start of the 1940s the stream of narrated films deepened into a flood; one might think that this turn to narration was just a fad, but the flood lasted throughout the decade without hint of abatement. Indeed, the 1940s were the technique's golden age, in terms of the sheer number of films that used it, the proportion of narrated to nonnarrated films, and the prestige, budget, and quality of those using narration.

Andrew Sarris correctly identifies one of the reasons for this golden age when he ascribes the new popularity of voice-over to the growth of screenwriters' power and prestige during the 1940s. In the 1930s writers had been exorbitantly paid, but allowed little authority or freedom; however, in the next decade, "As the Screenwriters' Guild achieved more authority and autonomy within the film industry, the word became the expressive equal of the image." [28] Moreover, during this decade, screenwriters such as Delmer Daves, Philip Dunne, John Huston, Joseph Mankiewicz, Abraham Polonsky, Robert Rossen, Preston Sturges, Orson Welles, and Billy Wilder took matters into their own hands by directing their own scripts.

It is no coincidence that these names all figure prominently on my filmography of narrated films. Although one can pick out certain screenwriters (for example, Howard Koch) who appear to have favored narration regardless of which director they were working with, and certain directors (for example, David Lean) who included narration regardless of their screenwriter(s), one must conclude that it always has been screenwriter-directors who have been most likely to use voice-over and to make it an integral part of their texts. This seems only fitting, because as screenwriters such directors are likely to eschew the traditional image bias and cherish verbal communication. Huston once remarked, "It seems to me . . . that the word contains as much action as a purely visual scene"; similarly, Welles has admitted, "I know that in theory the word is secondary in cinema but the secret of my work is that everything is based on the word. I do not make silent films. I must begin with what the characters say." [29] In their position as directors, Welles, Huston, Wilder, and others have been able to execute their verbally oriented screenplays.

Along with helping us detect the people who favored voice-over, the patterns emerging from the rich abundance of the 1940s enable us to see that the technique is intimately related to genre. Since every kind of film can, and sooner or later, does, use voice-over, my filmography of the decade ranges widely, yet it also shows distinct leanings towards four types of films: war films and semi-documentaries (which model their narration on that of newsreels and documentaries), and literary adaptations and *films noirs* (which owe debts to the novel and to radio dramas). There are reasons why these films figure so prominently during these years: Hollywood produced so many adaptations of British novels out of a wish to inspire or express solidarity with our beleaguered ally; semi-documentaries were created after film professionals returned from their service in government documentary units; *film noir* copied contemporary popular fiction and grew out of postwar unemployment, insecurity, and disillusionment. Yet as regards narration per se, cause and effect may be impossible to unsnarl. Were the 1940s voice-over's heyday because of some inherent proclivities of these dominant genres? Or did these genres embrace narration then primarily because of the converging influence of radio, literary, and documentary narration? Or was there some intangible forties Zeitgeist, some special feeling of loneliness and isolation, that the adaptations and *noirs* expressed with their intimate memoirs and confessions, and that the war films and semi-documentaries tried to assuage with their reassuring, authoritative pronouncements? At any rate, these four types of films (strictly speaking, "adaptations" do not constitute a "genre") have made voice-over a standard—though not invariant—element of their repertoires.

By the end of the 1940s, narrative cinema had established its own ways of handling voice-over, but the industry was not impervious to new outside influences.

Television and Postwar Documentaries

Radio continued to rely upon narration throughout the 1940s, but by the 1950s radio drama was on its way out, vanquished by television. Television embraced narration instantly, and, encountering relatively little critical resistance, has used it consistently ever since. For the most part, television copied its use of narration from its predecessors, but the new medium also established a few specific strategies to deal with its own formats and requirements.

Chief among these specific strategies is television's tendency to rely upon *on-screen* narrators. People on television talk straight at the camera all the time, and through it, straight to the viewer in his or her living room. Certainly the dramatic anthology series of the fifties relied upon on-camera "hosts"—for example, "Boris Karloff's Mystery Playhouse," "Robert Montgomery Presents Your Lucky Strike Theater," and "General Electric Theater" (hosted by Ronald Reagan)—and this practice has continued down through the years to Alistair Cooke on "Masterpiece Theater." Often all of the host's narration is done on-camera in introductory or concluding segments, but in some cases he or she would also narrate the body of the drama via voice-over.

With the replacement of the anthology series by prerecorded continuing series, television shows often found themselves with a problem: the need to give a capsule description of the program's premise (an abstract and orientation) to new viewers. Radio serials had faced the same problem, and thus had offered such openings as the following:

> And now, "Our Gal Sunday," the story of an orphan girl named Sunday, from the little town of Silver Creek, Colorado who in young womanhood married England's richest, most handsome lord, Lord Henry Grinthrope—the story that asks the question, can this girl from a mining town in the West find happiness as the wife of a wealthy and titled Englishman?[30]

While some television series have conveyed their situations and characters solely through visual montages, others turned to voice-over introductions, which, because they were repeated week after week, have become indelibly engrained in the nation's psyche. Try as one might, who can ever forget the openings of "Star Trek," "The Beverly Hillbillies," or "The Brady Bunch"?

The cinema has never needed to copy television's specific strategies, but one may intuit that television has nevertheless had a large indirect influence. The film industry has traditionally looked upon television as an adversary, and its response since the 1950s has been to offer gratifications unavailable on the intimate little screen—more sex and violence, more spectacular visual effects, wide-screen processes, 3-D, anything to make film grander, more exciting. Television's unhesitating embrace of narration did not reinforce filmic voice-over: on the contrary, as might have been expected, filmmakers eschewed a technique so utilized by their rival. Perhaps Alfred Hitchcock's case is paradigmatic: he hosted television shows for more than a decade, but never narrated his own films (though he does introduce *The Wrong Man* [1957]), and, in fact, avoided narration in his post-1950 works.

Television news programming quietly killed off newsreels and *The March of Time*, but documentaries survived, partially through television's sponsorship, partially despite it. In the late 1950s and early 1960s, spurred on by technological breakthroughs—lightweight 16mm cameras that could be handled by one person and portable Nagra tape decks—a new style of documentary filmmaking emerged both here and abroad. "Direct cinema" was born when documentarians such as Richard Leacock and the Maysles brothers took their equipment outside and used their improved mobility and sound-recording capabilities to record their subjects in situ, speaking for themselves.

One of the hallmarks of direct cinema, which strives for objectivity and immediacy, is an abhorrence of traditional voice-over commentary, which is thought to be elitist and authoritarian and to interfere with the viewer's experience of the film. Although documentaries with traditional voice-over tracks have continued to be made, and although many of the films of this school have themselves resorted to explanatory narration, Richard Leacock's, Albert and David Maysles', Don Pennybaker's, and Frederick Wiseman's documentaries were fresh and engrossing, and demonstrated how much could be conveyed without voice-over. Moreover, as discussed previously, their political/ideological quarrel with narration, echoed and expanded by the French, has been extremely influential.

Actually, the technological breakthroughs that led to direct cinema have also affected the entire spectrum of film and television. Independent films (that is, those produced outside a major studio) received a boost from the availability of cheaper, more convenient 16mm stock and cameras. And while the 35mm format continues as the standard for major theatrical releases, advances in audio technology—the coming of magnetic tape recorders and mixing apparatus after the war, the invention of crystal-controlled motors that keep the tape recorder and camera in sync without their needing to be physically connected, the refinement of bidirectional and unidirectional microphones designed to pick up only preselected sources, and later, the invention of radio microphones that allowed filmmakers to dispense wtih clumsy and limiting sound booms—have facilitated shooting in all sorts of locations. Although shooting synchronous sound on location will always entail difficulties with airplane, traffic, and crowd noises, most of the handicaps that encouraged, if not constrained, fiction films and documentaries alike to use narration over exterior scenes have been eliminated.

Fiction Films, 1950 to the Present

The principal 1940s genres that had adopted narration—*noir*, semi-documentaries, war films, and adaptations—spilled over into the 1950s. Domestic comedies (which were striving for a certain tongue-in-cheek aura) and extremely low-budget science-fiction films (which would try anything to straighten out their disjointed continuity) also began to use narration regularly. New screenwriter-directors such as Frank Tashlin joined the ranks of voice-over aficionados. This decade saw some of the more off-beat experiments: narration from beyond the grave (*Sunset Boulevard*), before birth (*The First Time* [Tashlin, 1952]), and by an Oscar statuette (*Susan Slept Here* [Tashlin, 1954]).

Nevertheless, in comparison with the 1940s, the flood of narrated films subsided. The studios were reeling from the disruption of the antitrust decrees, from television's inroads on their audiences, from the baby boom that moved families to the suburbs and kept them housebound, and from McCarthyite witch-hunting, which hit the screenwriting community particularly hard. Production as a whole declined, and narration, now a familiar, traditional technique, was either jazzed up or deemphasized in the scramble for exciting novelties such as 3-D or Odorama, which were supposed to turn the nightmare around.

But the slight drop off during the 1950s counts as nothing compared to the dearth of narrated films during the sixties and early seventies. Fewer and fewer films were produced all the time: *The Motion Picture Almanac* lists the average yearly output of ten major studios as 445 during the 1940s, 373 during the 1950s, and 163 during the 1960s. The statistics reflecting the status of screenwriters over this period are also revealing: in 1945, 490 writers were under contract to Hollywood studios; in 1950 there were only 67, and by 1960, only 48.[31] And because of the changes in the industry and in public taste, forties genres were in eclipse; the big commercial releases tended towards categories that had never found a niche for narration (for example, Broadway musicals) or towards genres that emphasized special effects and action at the expense of any type of dialogue (for example, spy/adventure films such as the James Bond series, and, later, disaster films). Of the blockbusters on which desperate producers gambled more and more, only the historical epics incorporated narration, and they used it in a rather pedestrian manner. Veteran screenwriter-directors continued to employ the technique at will, but the films of younger directors, such as Robert Altman, Sidney Lumet, Arthur Penn, and John Schlesinger, often strove for an almost documentary sense of immediacy and translucence. Thus, Altman's *noir,* his adaptation of Chandler's *The Long Goodbye* (1973), eschews narration.

Yet at the same time that narration was out of favor in the United States, it was being enthusiastically embraced in France. Narration has a long tradition in French cinema, having been frequently and thoughtfully employed by Sacha Guitry, Jean Cocteau, and Max Ophuls, among others. The New Wave directors were critics and/or screenwriters themselves, hardly hostile to allowing words to play a major role in their films, and many of their films are adaptations of novels or homages to traditional Hollywood genres, especially *film noir.* Moreover, as we all know, the thrust of this group was towards self-consciously analyzing and foregrounding, as opposed to effacing, their narrative techniques. The French New Wave's boundaries have been officially assigned as 1958–63, but from the films that are counted as "precursors" in the early 1950s (such as Robert Bresson's *Le Journal d'un curé de campagne* [1951]) to the more commercial releases of French directors in later years (which have had major American distribution), this movement is saturated with narration: look at many of Eric Rohmer's or Bresson's works, and practically any by Alain Resnais, François Truffaut, and Jean-Luc Godard. (*L'Année dernière à Marienbad* [1961], *Les Deux Anglaises et le continent* [1971], and *Deux ou trois choses que je sais d'elle* [1967] can serve as prime examples.) These directors and their less well-known colleagues Alain Robbe-Grillet, Chris Marker, and Marguerite Duras do not fall back on voice-over for convenience or merely to follow a convention, but weave it into their films' fabrics.[32]

From the late seventies onwards, there has been a new stirring in the American film industry. Directors and/or screenwriters such as Woody Allen, Francis Ford Coppola, Stanley Kubrick, Terence Malick, John Milius, Paul Schrader, and Martin Scorsese have been influenced both by the New Wave and by the film schools that some of them attended, and have been producing films that are both highly self-conscious in their use of cinematic techniques and marked by a certain personal expressiveness. In their films, from *A Clockwork Orange* (1971) to *Taxi Driver* (1976) to *Days of Heaven* (1978) and *Apocalypse Now* (1979), and through their influence, narration seems to have found new advocates and new audiences.

At present writing the use of narration is on a major upswing, not only in the films of the auteurs mentioned above, but, just as happened in the 1940s, in typical releases. Not surprisingly, as the filmography illustrates, many of the films now using narration are literary adaptations: *Sophie's Choice* (Pakula, 1982), *Heat and Dust* (Ivory, 1983); others imitate or parody *film noir: Blade Runner* (Scott, 1982), *Dead Men Don't Wear Plaid* (Reiner, 1982). Some, like Jamie Uys's *The Gods Must Be Crazy* (1980) satirize documentaries;

others, such as *The Big Red One* (Fuller, 1980) and *Platoon* (Stone, 1986), are serious war films. Epics, such as Sergio Leone's *Once Upon a Time in America* (1984) find narration useful, as do the spate of fantasy films exemplified by *Conan the Barbarian* (Milius, 1982). Comedies, such as Woody Allen's, are saturated with it. Television programs are going through their own narration revival, primarily due to the popularity of private eye shows such as "Magnum, P.I.," "Spencer for Hire," and "Mike Hammer." Even documentaries proper are returning to narration; in recent articles left-leaning critics have called on documentarians not to remain silent and hide behind a cloak of neutrality, but to provide leadership through open expression of their views in voice-over commentaries.[33]

But I believe the way narration is being used today differs from the way it was used in the 1940s. This difference lies in an increased tendency towards a deliberately nostalgic tone, a certain careful self-consciousness that often slides into overt parody. Whereas in forties films narration might imitate newsreels, documentaries, radio shows, or novels, in current releases the narration seems almost inescapably to refer us back to forties films. Narration now implies a hearkening back not so much to bygone days as to bygone films.

I draw several conclusions from this historical overview.

First, the course of development of cinematic narration (like the course of every aesthetic technique?) has been influenced both by the creativity and predilections of certain key individuals—such as Griffith, Lorentz, Welles, Leacock, Bresson, Godard, and Malick—and by the play of much larger forces—film technology, industry finances and power struggles, historical and social events. Since narration is somewhat dependent both on verbally oriented screenwriters and directors and on certain genres that have adopted the technique as their own, whatever forces have particularly affected the fortunes of these people and these genres have also particularly affected the fortunes of the technique. Unlike color cinematography, for instance, which is now such an industry standard that declining to use it makes a deliberate statement, narration has been and will remain a matter of choice, and thus subject to the winds of change and fashion.

Secondly, this overview should put to rest the charge that narration is a "literary" phenomenon and by implication inappropriate in film. Narration has been a component of the medium from its birth and is a major element of radio and television. For film to have adopted narration was more natural than for it to have abstained.

But this is not to deny that literary models have contributed to voice-over. A direct link indeed exists between the popular novels of the 1930s and 1940s and first-person voice-over. Adaptations of Eric Ambler's, James M. Cain's, or Raymond Chandler's novels rank among the most well known voice-over films of the forties (and Chandler, in fact, worked as a screenwriter on *Double*

Indemnity). Even *noirs* that came from original screenplays imitated the detective novels' distinctive narrative style.

More generally, film professionals and the American culture at large must have been influenced by the large role that first-person narration plays in Conrad and Fitzgerald, or that stream-of-consciousness plays in Joyce, Woolf, and Faulkner. It can hardly be just coincidence that after forty years of modernist literature's focus on chronology and narrative voice, the cinema, too, should depart from linearity and transparency. Faulkner, Fitzgerald, and West may not have worked on any particularly important voice-over films, but the fact that they were imported to Hollywood at all indicates the movie colony's reverence for literature (or high culture prestige).

But even though literature has undoubtedly been a major model for voice-over, we would do well to remember that the novel does not have a monopoly on narrative techniques. It is intriguing to note that the United States also witnessed a boom in stage narration during the 1930s, from the "Living Newspaper" productions of the Federal Theater Project during the early part of the decade to *Our Town* in 1938; meanwhile, abroad, Brecht continually experimented with epic theater. While Brechtian devices may seem rather removed from 1940s Hollywood, I would wager that (at least) most American screenwriters were well aware of contemporary drama; and certainly Brecht has had a direct influence on the French New Wave. Ultimately, film, radio, television, literature, and theater have undoubtedly all fed off one another in a complicated round-robin.

Finally, although I have presented the history of voice-over almost as a classic tale of birth, development, apogee, decline, and resurrection, looked at from another perspective, this history has been remarkably static. Almost all of the formal and tonal permutations: first person versus third, univocal versus polyvocal, absent narratee (receiver of the narrative) versus present narratee, poetry versus prose, authoritative versus lyrical, straight versus ironic, were present in nonfiction or fiction film by the mid to late 1930s. For the most part the contribution of succeeding decades has been in refining the techniques and integrating them in fictional contexts—in making the newborn baby breathe—rather than in breaking new ground. The only major exceptions are the question of the reliability of the narrator, a topic that did not become an issue until the mid forties, and which has loomed progressively larger ever since, and the question of the narrator's gender, which is only now beginning to be addressed.

Looking at these structural and tonal variables in detail is the task of the succeeding chapters.

3

First-Person Narrators

If you close your eyes and think back on movies you have seen, surely you can hear a sound montage of characters' voices. Marlowe fades in:

> The joint looked like trouble, but that didn't bother me. Nothing bothered me. The two twenties felt nice and snug against my appendix.

And then Scout,

> Maycomb was a tired old town in 1932 when I first knew it. . . . It was hotter then. A man's shirt collar was wilted by nine o'clock in the morning. . . .

And then Joe Gillis, Michael O'Hara, Mildred Pierce, Nick Carraway, Addie Ross, Jane Eyre, and Travis Bickle. Their voices are a major component of our cinematic heritage.

First-person narration is the more common form of voice-over in fiction films, cropping up in every genre, from Westerns to comedies, from cartoons to science fiction. In particular, however, it is a staple in literary adaptations and *films noirs*. We shall see that such narration can serve a variety of functions, including recreating/referring to a novel's narrative voice, conveying expositional information, and aiding in the presentation of complex chronologies. We shall also see that this type of narration can greatly affect the viewer's experience of the text by "naturalizing" the source of the narrative, by increasing identification with the characters, by prompting nostalgia, and by stressing the individuality and subjectivity of perception and storytelling.

Orson Welles called his radio series "First Person Singular." This label is both dead right and dead wrong for first-person films: their narration is singularly bewitching . . . partly because it is always plural.

Genette's Taxonomy of Narrators

Before proceeding, a pause for terminological and structural precision. Although we are all quite familiar with the term "first-person" narrator, at least since Booth raised objections to it in *The Rhetoric of Fiction,* we have realized that it is imprecise and misleading. As Gérard Genette notes in *Narrative Discourse:* "The narrator can be in his narrative (like every subject of an enunciating in his enunciated statement) *only* in the 'first person.' . . . The novelist's choice . . . is not between two grammatical forms, but between two narrative postures (whose grammatical forms are simply an automatic consequence), to have the story told by one of its 'characters' or to have it told by a narrator outside of the story." Genette labels narrators who are characters in the story they relate "homodiegetic" (they are of the same order, "homogeneous" with the "diegesis," the world of the story; narrators who are not characters— third-person narrators—he rechristens "heterodiegetic." [1]

All the narrators mentioned above are characters. But because many texts contain stories "embedded" within other stories like so many Russian dolls or Chinese boxes, one must also determine from which "narrative level" the narrator speaks. Genette thus teaches us to distinguish between narrators of the first level (the frame story), embedded narrators who tell a story-within-a-story, and doubly embedded narrators of a story-within-a-story-within-a-story. (Genette labels these narrators "extradiegetic," "intradiegetic," and "metadiegetic" respectively, but since "framing" and "embedded" are acceptably descriptive, I see no need to adopt those terms here.) Figure 1 helps one conceptualize these relationships.

Accordingly, one can classify narrators along not one, but two axes (Figure 2).

One problem with Genette's system is that his terms are tongue-twisting and obscure to the uninitiated. Another is that unless one keeps his criteria firmly in mind, confusion can reign. For instance, although Scheherazade is a character in the frame story, *The Arabian Nights,* as a narrator she is heterodiegetic because she does not figure as a character in the stories she relates; on the other hand, even though she is exterior to the stories she tells, she counts as an embedded narrator in relation to the text as a whole. But Genette's system makes up for these drawbacks by enabling one to draw important distinctions.

It would seem to be a simple matter to substitute examples of voice-over narrators in the chart above. Concentrating, for now, on character-narrators, Scout in Robert Mulligan's *To Kill a Mockingbird* (1962) could be termed a frame narrator; Philip Marlowe in *Murder, My Sweet* is embedded within the frame of the film as a whole; Norman Clyde in John Brahm's *The Locket* (1946) could even exemplify a doubly embedded narrator. All are participants in the stories they relate, but differ in where, how, and to whom they narrate.

Yet Genette's system was designed for literary narratives. Does the same breakdown of narrative levels hold true for film?

Figure 1

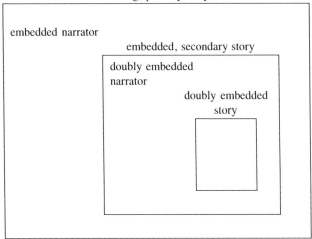

frame
narrator

Figure 2

Narrative Level

Relationship	framing	embedded
heterodiegetic	anonymous narrator of *The Arabian Nights*	Scheherazade
homodiegetic	Pip in *Great Expectations*	Magwitch

SOURCE: Adapted from Gérard Genette, *Narrative Discourse: An Essay in Method*, trans. Jane E. Lewin (Ithaca, N.Y.: Cornell Univ. Press, 1980), p. 248.

Who Really Narrates?

In literature, and consequently in most writings on narrative theory, we are accustomed to consider the narrator as either the speaker or the mediator (i.e., recorder) of every moment of the story. But a first-person voice-over narrator speaks intermittently—and sometimes only minimally—and is not in control of his or her story to the same degree, or in the same manner, as a literary narrator. Voice-over narration is just one of many elements, including musical scoring, sound effects, editing, lighting, and so on, through which the cinematic text is narrated.

Thus, along with critics such as Edward Branigan, Tony Pipolo, and Ellen Feldman,[2] I believe that behind the voice-over narrator there is another presence that supplements the nominal narrator's vision, knowledge, and storytelling powers. This presence is the narrating agent of all films (with or without voice-over). Such narrating agents are difficult to define, yet as Christian Metz argues in an oft-quoted passage: "The impression that *someone is speaking* is bound not to the empirical presence of a definite, known, or knowable speaker but to the listener's spontaneous perception of the linguistic nature of the object to which he is listening; because it is speech, someone must be speaking." Because narrative films are narrative, someone must be narrating. As Metz puts it: "The spectator perceives images which have obviously been selected (they could have been other images) and arranged (their order could have been different). In a sense, he is leafing through an album of predetermined pictures, and it is not he who is turning the pages but some 'master of ceremonies,' some 'grand image-maker.'"[3]

At present, there is no agreement on what to call this narrating agent. Following Bill Nichols,[4] I used one of the more common candidates, "voice," in my introduction, but surely Nick Browne is right when he stresses the "basic dis-analogy between the camera and narrative 'voice.'"[5] On the other hand, although people frequently use "camera" to refer to this agency (to wit, "the 'camera' cuts from X to Y"), the term is misleading in that the film is narrated not only by what the literal camera does and does not do, but also by editing, lighting, graphics, processing, staging, and the sound track. "Implied author," Feldman's choice, risks confusion with the literary use of the term, where it refers not to a narrating agency but to the moral/ideological image of the author projected by the text. "Implied director" and "implied narrator" both have advantages, but the former makes auteurist assumptions, and the latter does not serve me here because it risks confusion with voice-over narrators. A term without preexisting connotations would be best, but I hesitate to propose a neologism not already in wide currency. If one returns then, to the seminal and widely known paragraph from Metz quoted above, one has the choice between "master of ceremonies," which is sexist and circusy, and "grand image-maker," which slights the sound track. I here choose the second because shorn of the too-colorful adjective, "image-maker" clearly captures the activity of the off-screen presence—making images—where "making" is broad enough to encompass all the selecting, organizing, shading, and even passive recording processes that go into the creation of a narrative sequence of images and sounds. The bias of "image-maker" towards the visual track is slightly advantageous in this context because it provides a clearer contrast to the aural voice-over narrators; however, one should keep in mind that the image-maker is also the maker/conveyor of all dialogue, sound effects, and music.

Thus, if behind the voice-over narrator one can always find the real narrator, the image-maker, and distinguish (in Feldman's revealing phrase) *another level of narrative,* voice-over narrators could never actually occupy the catbird seat, could never be responsible for the primary diegesis. They are always embedded within the image-maker's discourse. In Dickens' *Great Expectations* Pip is a frame narrator, but in Lean's version, even though we never see Pip narrating, the voice we hear is not the autonomous and consistent mediator of the story, but rather an embedded narrator relayed to us by the image-maker.

And yet, in many cases the voice-over narrator is so inscribed in the film as to seem as if he or she has generated not only what he is saying but also what we are seeing. In other words, films often create the sense of character-narration so strongly that one accepts the voice-over narrator as if he or she were the mouthpiece of the image-maker either for the whole film or for the duration of his or her embedded story. We put our faith in the voice not as created but as creator.

In the final analysis, the structure of each film (and the predispositions of each viewer) influence whether the viewer suspends disbelief and accepts the pose of the voice-over. In weighing each case, Feldman would have us consider "the frequency of [the character's] narration, the kind and degree of co-ordination between the first-person narration and the represented action of the narrative, and the method used to imply that the represented action is the 'product' of the narration." [6] Although Feldman has identified the relevant variables, I believe that she reverses the order of their importance.

The single most crucial factor in our acceptance of the pose is that the film emphasize the character's claim to be telling the story. This connection can be forged in several ways: through showing the character in the act of narrating, through the narrator explicitly telling us that this is his or her story (that is, by the voice providing us a Labovian abstract and/or orientation), or through a combination of conventional indicators such as the camera dollying or zooming in on the character's face and the image dissolving to another scene, often to the accompaniment of dreamy music. Brian Henderson claims that films redundantly pile up these indicators in order to signal time shifts;[7] actually, it is not, or not only, the chronological liberty that needs to be so loudly trumpeted, but the figurative switch in narrating agents. In order for us to suspend disbelief, the film must tie the story to the character—the tighter, the better.

But frequency of narration per se does not make that much difference; voice-over is like strong perfume—a little goes a long way. Critics charge that voice-over preludes that anchor a film to a character who never narrates again, as in Hitchcock's *Rebecca* (1940), are a cheap trick for creating instant nostal-

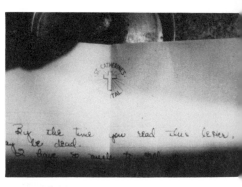

Letter from an Unknown Woman. Stefan's first glance at letter.

Lisa's letter—no voice-over

As Stefan begins to read letter intently, the camera dollies in; the picture dissolves and then clears.

Lisa [voice-over]: By the time you read this letter, I may be dead. I have so much to tell you and perhaps so very little time. Will I ever send it? I don't know. I must find the strength to write now before it's too late. And as I write it may become clear that what happened to us had its own reason beyond our poor understanding. If this reaches you, you'll know how I became yours when you didn't even know who I was, or even that I existed.

I think everyone has two birthdays, the day of his physical birth and the beginning of his conscious life.

gia. The trick may be cheap but it is also completely effective. More narration would keep our attention focused on the narrator rather than the action, but would not be responsible for establishing the pose that the film is Mrs. De Winter's personal story, not an objective account from a removed image-maker. As Eric Smoodin puts it, "Once the presence of the voice-over narrator has been established, the entire film serves as a sort of linguistic event, as the narrator's speech even when there is none." [8]

Finally, the question of the degree of correspondence between the narration and the represented action brings us to difficult issues concerning "point of view." Theorists have sometimes assumed that for a character to be accepted as a narrator, the filmmakers must consistently shoot from that character's physical point of view, as Robert Montgomery does in the famous *Lady in the Lake* (1946). But Genette argues that there is always a distinction between "who sees?" (i.e., who serves as motivation for the physical—and figurative—"point of view"?) and "who speaks?" (i.e., who is the narrator?). In their rethinking and redefining of "point of view" as "focalization," Genette and his followers have shown that literary narrators have a multitude of choices as to how to "focalize" their texts: focalization can be congruent with narration or discongruent; it can be "fixed," "variable," or "multiple"; it entails both a subject (the focalizer) and an object (the focalized); the focalizer can be internal or external to the diegesis; the objects of focalization can be seen from the "inside" (i.e., privileged access to their thoughts and feelings) or only from the outside. Thus, focalization is "internal" and "fixed" through little Maisie in *What Maisie Knew,* but she is not the narrator; she "sees," but an anonymous third-person narrator "speaks." Focalization and narration alternate together between four different characters in *The Sound and the Fury;* and *Middlemarch,* consistently narrated by one anonymous voice, varies its subjects and objects of focalization from scene to scene or paragraph to paragraph, sometimes revealing characters' thoughts and feelings (focalization "from within"), sometimes viewing them from the outside (focalization "from without"). [9]

This is not the place for working out all the ramifications of focalization for film (and actually the concept has itself come under criticism for its inconsistencies), but we should realize that when film critics call for the camera to assume the narrator's physical point of view, they are not actually discussing *narration.* Instead, they are asking for rigid focalization through the eyes of the character à la *Lady in the Lake.* But in fact, Genette notes that in literature, such rigid focalization is extremely rare—even when narrators focalize their texts through the eyes of their character-I (that is, their own younger persona within the story world), they sooner or later depart to a greater or lesser degree from that character's angle of vision. Nor is such rigid focalization necessary. Homodiegetic narrators may focalize their texts through anyone they choose at any given point without indiscretion. Tristram Shandy, after all, uses Uncle Toby as a medium for recounting events that he himself could not have seen, events that took place before he was born.

Recent studies of "suture" and point-of-view shots have demonstrated that films generally shift their focalization quite fluidly, now placing the camera approximately in the position of one character, now moving it to the reverse angle, now placing it in the position of some imaginary perfect observer, now placing it in some improbable, inhuman position.[10] When we accept a voice-over narrator as if he or she were the voice of the image-maker, it is only fair to allow that narrator the same flexibility of focalizaton (or, in Nick Browne's terms, "surrogation") that we typically allow silent image-makers. Thus, shots of the character himself (the character-I) do not violate our contract with the voice (the narrating-I); neither does the presentation of scenes in which the character-I is absent. Only in a film such as Preminger's *Laura,* which abruptly both stops using Waldo Lydecker's voice-over *and* shifts from closely following his activities to centering around his antagonist, the detective Mark McPherson, does the inconsistency trigger the viewer's doubts regarding the purported narrator's position and control.

In terms of figurative point of view, one often notes that aspects of the scenic presentation comment upon or qualify the voice-over narrator's statements, implying that the image-maker knows more than the voice. In fact, the image-maker has varied and powerful tools at his disposal to undercut the voice-over narrator's statements at the very moment they are made. Thus, in certain cases, discussed in chapter 5, if the narrator's commentary and the image-maker's scenic presentation are disparate enough, the viewer will gradually nullify his or her contract with the narrating voice and realize that the story is actually being presented by a wiser, heterodiegetic image-maker.

But in general, there are powerful inducements for viewers to bend over backwards to accept the voice-over as the teller of the film. Depending upon the talent, aims, and artistic control of the filmmakers, image-makers can have strong presences and individual "personalities"—the *auteur* theory, among other things, has focused our attention on the distinctive "Hitchcockian" or "Fordian" narrating presences. But even at his most manifest, the image-maker is an odd, bodiless construction, difficult to assimilate to the rest of our experience of narratives and narrators (and thus some critics, such as David Bordwell, object to any anthropomorphizing of filmic narration).[11] As Elizabeth W. Bruss has stated: "It is doubtful that the effects of shooting, editing and staging are capable of expressing what we conventionally call 'personality' to the degree that language can."[12] Voice-over narration has been used in so many films precisely in order to "naturalize" the strangeness of the image-maker, to link filmic narration to everyday, dinner-time storytelling. As critics we may be skeptical and vigilant, but as spectators, we tumble for the ruse again and again.

To summarize, a homodiegetic voice-over narrator is always subsumed by and thus subordinate to a more powerful narrating agent, the image-maker who dramatizes the story on the screen. But as viewers, we are generally eager to overlook the less definable, less familiar image-maker, and unless the film plays upon the distinction and deliberately frustrates us, we embrace the character as the principal storyteller. We then allow the character a wide latitude of powers, almost as if he or she had been crowned image-maker for a day.

The Circumstances of Narration

If we accept the voice-over narrator's pose as the teller of his tale, then we must decide from which narrative level the voice speaks. Determining narrative level is not just of theoretical importance. One's expectations about, and experience of, a narrator hinge upon his or her position. Frame narrators are conventionally given the greatest authority and allowed the greatest freedoms; contrarily, we are more likely to be skeptical about the veracity or impartiality of narrators when we see them in the act of narrating and can judge their stories against material openly presented by an overarching image-maker.

Furthermore, I believe that one might usefully supplement Genette's model with a distinction between two types of embedded narrators. A difference exists between an embedded narrator whose story takes up nearly all of the text and is surrounded by a slender frame (such as Nelly Dean in Brontë's *Wuthering Heights*) and a narrator who merely fills us in on some isolated past event, recounts a dream, or provides entertainment (such as Tweedledee in *Through the Looking Glass,* who recites "The Walrus and the Carpenter" to Alice). The quantitative difference becomes qualitative: the first narrator plays a much larger role in the mediation of the story and consequently has important functions in the text as a whole; the latter serves more as an isolated interlude. Thus I propose we distinguish a subset of embedded narrators by referring to them as micro-narrators. Determining the boundaries of this subset presents difficulty; I would choose to define micro-narrators rather narrowly as those speakers whose story comprises less than 25 percent of the entire text. Thus Don Lockwood in *Singin' in the Rain* (Donen and Kelly, 1952), who briefly—and totally unreliably—narrates the story of his rise to stardom, is a micro-narrator whose narration is less central to his film than, say Mildred's is to *Mildred Pierce* (Curtiz, 1945). Because they occupy this marginal position, micro-narrators are the least powerful and the easiest to compromise.

In many films the voice-over's status as embedded narrator is unequivocal; the text starts independently of voice-over, and then, at some later point in the action, a character sits down to tell a story. A good example can be found in Huston's *The Man Who Would Be King* (1975) where Peachy (Michael Caine) comes to Kipling (Christopher Plummer) one evening to tell him the story of his grisly adventure with Danny. But in certain films a difficulty arises in determining whether the voice-over belongs to a frame or embedded narrator. Novels can and do open with a voice and a figurative "blank screen": "You don't know about me without you have read a book by the name of *The Adventures of Tom Sawyer*" introduces us to Huck as narrator before presenting anything of story time or story place. But films conventionally start with something on the screen, and thus instantly throw us into a story world conveyed by the image-maker. Even in the case of a film such as Woody Allen's *Annie Hall,* which starts with Alvy Singer on a limbo set speaking directly to the camera and thus establishes the narrator before moving into the story proper, once we see Alvy Singer on the screen his narration becomes overtly embedded within the image-maker's discourse of images. Accordingly, we find it easiest to accept voice-over narrators as primary, framing storytellers when the voice-over is simultaneous with the film's opening shots, when one has seen as little as possible of the story world, and certainly before one sees the narrating character. If this occurs, viewers can believe that the images have been created by the unseen voice, rather than the voice by the image-maker.

Literary theorist Bertil Romberg calls the host of circumstances surrounding the narrator's narrating instance his or her "epic situation." [13] Frame narrators, by definition, narrate from some point in time (and space) outside of the story boundaries. We usually are given very little information concerning their situation, though on occasion we can determine whether it is a matter of years' remove from the story or whether narration starts when the story ends. These narrators either speak to an unspecified audience or address us viewers directly and self-consciously. Direct address can offer a special intimacy between the narrator and the viewer, an intimacy that screenwriters and directors know how to exploit to great advantage. Following Anthony Burgess's practice in the novel, Kubrick, for instance, makes *A Clockwork Orange* doubly disturbing by having the ultra-violent Alec (Malcolm McDowell) constantly refer to himself as "your friend and humble narrator" and to the audience as "oh my brothers and only friends," thus implicating us in his world and his value system.

On the other hand, with an embedded narrator the audience is automatically acquainted with the time, place, and manner of storytelling and with the narrating character's motivation. Often these characters speak in confession or reflection-inspiring locales, such as police stations, prisons, churches, deathbeds, and graveyards (or just in front of mirrors); and they commonly offer their stories to listeners such as priests, journalists, psychiatrists, policemen, and juries—people to whom they feel bound to explain the whole story. [14] These narratees in the frame story serve as audience surrogates, reacting to the story, but we viewers are given even more opportunity to judge, since unlike the fictional listeners we are outside the diegesis, invisible and superior to the narrating character, eavesdropping.

The issue of "to whom is the narrator speaking?" leads us to a hallmark of

Opening of *A Clockwork Orange*

voice-over narration. One must recognize that the voice-over narrator is always speaking to someone, whether that someone is the theater audience, a dramatized narratee, or just himself, and that his act of telling a story out loud couches the filmic story as a deliberate, conscious communication. Thus a film with voice-over differs from a non-narrated film in which the characters are conventionally oblivious to the camera's and spectators' presence, and we are in the position of spying on their activities. If Laura Mulvey and her followers are right in their argument that the pleasure of the classic Hollywood film is predicated on a certain voyeuristic thrill,[15] voice-over narration is a mechanism for assuaging the guilt involved by such voyeurism. One is no longer spying on unconscious characters. Instead, the tale is being deliberately addressed to us, or—at worst—we are overhearing a tale deliberately addressed to another. Even in the latter case, however, we know that the narrating character is not being caught totally off-guard. Perhaps this attribute of voice-over narration explains why it is generally eschewed by certain directors (such as Hitchcock in his later films and Brian De Palma) and certain genres ("slasher" and horror films) that want to explore or exploit the dynamics of voyeurism.

Another facet of a narrator's situation involves his purported narrative medium. Romberg finds that the great majority of first-person novels pose their narrators as writers of one type or another, and couch their tales as "having-been-written," as opposed to being told aloud or merely "thought."[16] Romberg's insight leads him into discussing the way the narrator's status as author leads to typical novel formats: the memoir novel, the diary novel, and the epistolary novel.

Type of Text	Author	Reader	Voice-over
Kind Hearts and Coronets memoir	Mazzini	Mazzini	Mazzini
Missing diary	Charles	Beth	Beth
Letter from an Unknown Woman letter	Lisa	Stefan	Lisa

Which media do voice-over narrators favor? How do they couch their stories? Often audiences are supposed to accept the stories as "having-been-written." Frame narrators of adaptations often speak in conjunction with shots of pages from their novels, and embedded narrators often present their stories as memoirs, diaries, or letters. Such anchoring of the voice-over to *writing* constitutes yet another reason why voice-over is so often categorized as a "literary technique." But it is curious that in most films the narrators are either not currently in the act of writing or not the authors of the stories. In other words, such flashbacks have two epic situations: their original written composition and their oral reading aloud; it is by means of the second that they figure in the film. (As the table above indicates, the voice-over can belong to either the writer or the reader.) With frame narrators of adaptations, even though we see pages from the novel and recognize that they are supposed to be in the midst of writing their autobiographies, because we actually hear their voices, instead of just seeing silent titles, it feels as if the written texts have thrown off their inky cloaks and reverted to what has been termed the most fundamental epic situation: "a narrator present[ing] a story orally to a listening public." [17]

In fact, voice-over films will go to all sorts of lengths to create oral epic situations. The modification of *Double Indemnity* may be emblematic: in the novel Walter Neff writes his memoir, in the film he dictates it into a dictaphone. Even when the epic situation is unspecified and no clues are dropped about the mode of narration, because we hear the narrator's voice, we think of him or her as transmitting the story orally.

A significant asymmetry appears here. If it is most common and feels most "natural" for first-person narrators of novels to have written their stories down—thus forging a match between the narrative pose and the actual textual medium, then one might expect that the most common pose for a voice-over narrator would be "filmmaker." However, because of the strangeness and ambiguity involved in "telling a film," it is extremely rare for a homodiegetic narrator to encourage us to believe that he or she is narrating through celluloid. In mainstream American cinema, *Sunset Boulevard,* narrated by a screenwriter who makes one self-conscious reference to the narrative's status as film, may be the only (minimal) case; one has to look further afield to independent or foreign films for additional examples.* Not the least major effect of using voice-over is that, instead of emanating from an undefinable blend of script, direction, acting, and technical wizardry, the story seems simply to spring from a person speaking aloud.

Story and Discourse and
How Green Was My Valley

Non-voice-over films are narrated, but their image-makers' nonverbal narration is not as conspicuous as voice-over; indeed one of the hallmarks of the classic Hollywood style has been to make the narration invisible and promote the illusion that one is watching an unmediated reality. By making the "voice" more obvious and exploitable, voice-over films highlight the double-layering effect discussed by narrative theorists—the text can now clearly be seen as the interplay between the narrative action, the story, and the process of telling it, the discourse. The character who narrates is also doubled, inhabiting the story as the experiencing-I while providing the discourse as narrating-I.

Furthermore, as Christian Metz notes, "One of the functions of narrative is to invent one time scheme in terms of another time scheme." And it is precisely the duality of story and discourse that "renders possible all the temporal distortions that are commonplace in narratives." [18] Of course, even without oral narration, films can and do create complex chronologies, so much so that *flashback* and *flashforward* have been adopted by literary theorists. Inasmuch as certain temporal relationships can be conveyed through verbal tense structure more precisely or more economically than through "tenseless" visual images, the addition of a spoken narration track only greases the wheels, only increases a film's opportunities to manipulate chronology. Thus voice-over films can flash forward with "prophetic narratives" of what a character is going to do (e.g., in Preston Sturges's *The Lady Eve* [1941] Joan anticipates the moment of Charles's proposal: "One day, two weeks from now, we'll be riding in the hills . . . and the sunset will be so beautiful I'll be overcome and have to get off my horse to admire it"); they can indicate synchronicity between discourse and story (as in the present-tense opening of Anthony Mann's *Raw Deal* [1948], where Pat begins, "This is the day, this is the day, the last time I shall drive up to these gates, these iron bars that keep the man I love

---

*See, for instance, Nagisa Oshima's *The Man Who Left His Will on Film* or Jim McBride's *David Holzman's Diary.*

locked away from me"); and they can not only flashback at will, but also precisely locate story time by a simple phrase (e.g., in Robert Wise's *House on Telegraph Hill* [1951]: "My story begins eleven years ago and two thousand miles away in my native Poland").

The above examples all pertain to the "order" in which the discourse presents the events of the story. As Eric Smoodin also demonstrates,[19] voice-over is also useful in conveying Genette's categories of "frequency" and "duration." Thus, for instance, voice-over is a handy means of communicating that a certain event took place several times, as when in *Letter from an Unknown Woman,* Lisa notes that "Night after night [she] returned to the same spot." It also is perfect for compressing story events, as in Herbert Biberman's *Salt of the Earth* (1954) where Esperanza tells us, "Ramon was in the hospital for a week. And then in jail for 30 days for assault."

It is by exploiting the double-layer of story and discourse, the dual status of the narrating character, and this ease of temporal manipulation, that first-person voice-over has found one of its major missions: couching a film as a remembrance of things past. Certainly flashbacks (which have been used since the early days of filmmaking, but figure so prominently during the 1940s) and voice-over fit together like hand in glove. Michael Wood has written: "The flashback of the Forties and Fifties was . . . a compulsion, the instrument of a constant, eager plunging into the past. A slow, misty dissolve, and off we went into the day before yesterday, when things were different; into a time before all this (whatever *all this* might be in any given movie) happened to us."[20] What exactly prompted this constant, eager plunging into the past is obscure—the war and postwar disillusionment perhaps, or resistance to the dizzying pace of technological progress and upheaval, or maybe the example of modernist literature's yen for temporal experimentation. At any rate, in scores of films (many of them literary adaptations), the voice-over is used both to move us into the past "when things were different" and to create a contrast to the present: the story's significance is only clear in relation to the discourse-now. At the same time, the voice-over is employed to make the viewer compare the youthful or unworldly experiencing-I and the older and wiser narrating-I, in other words, to detail an innocent's coming to knowledge from his or her grownup perspective.

How Green Was My Valley not only provides a perfect example, but, since it was made in 1941, may well have set the mold. The film adapts Richard Llewellyn's novel recounting the life of a Welsh boy, Huw Morgan, and manages to remain generally faithful to its source, despite a great deal of compression. It dwells on the warmth of the Morgan family life and the destruction of that family, its community, and its environment because of the exploitative practices of the mine owners. Huw's father and eldest brother are killed in mining accidents, his other older brothers emigrate in search of greater opportunity, his sister's romance is thwarted, and his once beautiful valley is despoiled by the effluences of the coal mine.

The history of the production provides an interesting example of voice-over as forethought.[21] The producer, Darryl Zanuck (himself an erstwhile screenwriter), had the technique in mind from the beginning of the project. He wrote to the first screenwriter, Ernest Pascal:

> I think we should take a revolutionary viewpoint of the screenplay of this story and we should tell it as the book does—through the eyes of Huw, the little boy. We should do much of the picture with him as an off-stage commentator, with many of the scenes running silent and nothing but his voice over them. And then, of course from time to time we will let the voice dissolve into scenes.
>
> If we use this technique we can capture much of the wonderful descriptive dialogue of the book, particularly when the boy talks about the valley and about his father and mother.[22]

Zanuck later hired Philip Dunne as screenwriter and William Wyler as director (Wyler had used voice-over in *Wuthering Heights* in 1939); Dunne and Wyler cast the film and worked on the set design. But the New York office of Twentieth Century–Fox raised objections and the project was presumed dead, so Wyler went on to other commitments. John Ford—a natural replacement because he had just had a great success with another film about laboring people, *The Grapes of Wrath*—was hired a few months later when he promised to bring the film in on a budget of a million dollars.

Dunne records that he felt the property called for narration, that it was useful in compressing a very long novel into movie length, and that, following Sturges's lead with *The Power and the Glory,* he called the technique "narratage." Although he recalls that Wyler had some influence on the script, Ford requested only minor adjustments and then proceeded to shoot it as written.* Ford's own talents and interests lay in another direction. Ford once told Peter Bogdanovich: "There's no such thing as a good script really. Scripts are dialogue, and I don't like all that *talk*. I've always tried to get things across visually."[23] Ford's contribution was to use his skill with actors, his feel for gestures and staging, and his unique eye for composition and camera movement to imbue the script with meaning and emotion, to make the words reso-

---

*Once when Dunne visited the set, Ford teased him by having the entire cast and crew line up and chant to the tune of "The Farmer in the Dell":

> We haven't changed a line,
> We haven't changed a line,
> It's just the way you wro-ote it,
> We haven't changed a line.

(Philip Dunne, *Take Two: A Life in Movies and Politics* [New York: McGraw-Hill, 1980], p. 100.)

nate over shots that extend and amplify their meaning, in short, to create an image-maker who brings Huw's story to life. (Because neither Ford nor Dunne were involved in post-production, the recording of the narration track and the film's final cut were supervised by its editor, Barbara McLean, and, one would surmise, Zanuck.[24])

The film opens with a shot of a man from the chest down, standing behind a table, packing a few items in a cloth; meanwhile we hear:

> I am packing my belongings in the shawl my mother used to wear when she went to the market, and I am going from my valley and this time I shall never return. I am leaving behind me my fifty years of memory.[25]

The camera immediately pans through the window; a series of shots shows us a dismal town, inhabited by elderly, joyless people (with a close-up of one old woman—"Fate," "Death," "Sorrow"?—who gazes off reflectively). A mountainous coal slag heap looms over the houses. The voice goes on:

> Memory. Strange that the mind will forget so much of what only this moment has passed, and yet hold clean and bright the memory of what happened years ago, of men and women long since dead. Who shall say what is real and what is not?
>
> Can I believe my friends all gone, when their voices are still a glory in my ears? No! and I will stand to say no, and no again, for they remain a living truth within my mind. There is no fence nor hedge around time that is gone. You can go

> back and have what you like of it, if you can remember; so I can close my eyes on
> my valley as it is today and it is gone, and I see it as it was when I was a boy.

Here the picture dissolves from a shot of the valley crowded with ugly buildings, to a shot of lush and sunny hills.

> Green it was, and possessed of the plenty of the earth. In all Wales there was
> none so beautiful.

Such an opening amounts to what William Labov would term an extended
abstract, stating not only what this film is about, but why it is being recounted—namely, to tell us about the valley's lost beauty and to illustrate the
redemptive powers of memory. Note, too, the tie-in between the film's title
and the narrator's explicit reference to the "greenness" (i.e., the youth, vi-
tality, and naturalness) of the valley. When, as here, a voice-over narrator refers to the title of the text, the viewer's belief in the narrator's power and control is intensified, and endowing him with image-maker status becomes that
much easier.

Moreover, the film starts at "narrating time," but this time has purposely
been left unspecified. All we can gather is that it is some forty years or so after
the story events. Judging by the voice, Huw is a middle-aged man, yet the
filmmakers never show his face; leaving him faceless and mysterious leaves
the viewer unsure whether he is a frame or embedded narrator. We are not
given any information about Huw's epic situation or encouraged to analyze
the circumstances surrounding his storytelling. Rather, the filmmakers start
at Huw's narrating-now primarily to illustrate the contrast between narrating
place and story place, between the valley debased and the green valley of
memory, and to emphasize the quantity of time between narrating-now and
story-now.

Having flashed back to the time of his childhood, the grown-up voice continues talking to us, now providing an extended "orientation." Among the
most common tasks of voice-over narrators is to introduce the characters of
the story and to define story time and story place. Huw's first duty is to introduce "himself"—after all, how do we know to whom the unseen voice wafting in on the sound track belongs? To be pragmatic, if we are familiar with an
actor from previous moviegoing, we have no difficulty attaching the recognized voice to the character that actor plays. In cases where the voice is not
familiar (as here), we have learned to assign it to the first plausible on-screen
candidate.* In *How Green Was My Valley*, the first shot of the flashback

---

*Some films toy with our desire to pin the disembodied voice to a character in the story. Raoul
Walsh's *Battle Cry* (1955) begins with a close-up of a marine recruiting poster with a life-size
marine staring straight at the camera. "They call me 'Mac,'" says a male voice off-screen: the
implication is that the narrator is the marine in the poster, and thus, metaphorically, "the voice of

shows a young boy walking with an older man while the narrator talks about his relationship with his father. The narrator does not have to state, "This is me," the viewer automatically makes the connection between the voice and the child on the screen. In this and other adaptations of bildungsromans, the theoretical split between the narrating-I and the experiencing-I is made flesh, since the two personae are literally two different people, one played by a grownup (Irving Pichel) and one by a child actor (Roddy McDowell).

Huw not only goes on to introduce all the other major characters, but describes a way of life to the viewer. He goes through all the family rituals: his father and brothers coming home with their pay; washing off the coal dust; family mealtimes; the allotment of spending money. Moreover, he describes these actions as iterative (e.g., "Someone *would* strike up a song and the valley *would* ring with the sound of many voices . . .") with much more ease than could be accomplished solely through visual means. And the image-maker collaborates with the narrator. As J. A. Place notes, throughout this section we hear only the barest bits of dialogue, and noises such as Huw's sister Angharad's call and the clink of the coin in the plate sound exaggerated.[26] The carefully composed long-shots, the characters' slow movements, and the musical scoring help to make this orientation seem timeless, like shots in a picture album. All this stylization reflects the correspondence between the narration and represented action. This image-maker creates no disparities between the narration and the rest of the text; in every instance the former substantiates, and, in fact, amplifies, the latter's claims. We are thus fully convinced that we are perceiving the story through Huw's memory.

Throughout this section, and indeed throughout the film, the voice stresses his identity with the child on the screen ("I am the child that was," he explicitly reminds us), yet emphasizes his distance in time. When the boy goes to buy toffee, the narrator remarks that the taste "is with me now, so many years later. It makes me think of so much that was good that is gone." Such comments recall the bleak opening section and tinge the happy scenes with foreboding. In fact, every moment of the story is clouded by our knowledge of the future, and thus flavored by a bittersweet nostalgia.

With the arrival of Bronwyn, Huw's future sister-in-law, on a visit one Saturday afternoon, the voice-over gives way to synchronous dialogue, and the iterative description gives way to what Labov terms narrative action. Brian Henderson calls this moment "a fall into time: out of the frequentive mode, which is preserved, as in Proust, from the ravages of time, into the singulative mode, the order of irreversible time and change, in which the family will be

---

the marines." But Mac turns out to be a character, a marine communications officer played by James Whitmore, who enters the action about midway through, and yet never quite sheds his symbolic identity. This delay in identifying the narrator is even more pronounced in some more recent films. For other examples, see *The Road Warrior* (Miller, 1982) and *Conan the Barbarian* (Milius, 1982).

dispersed and the valley destroyed." [27] The body of the film progresses with relatively little narration, though the voice does return to summarize events. For example, the narrator tells us,

> Twenty-two weeks the men were out, as the strike moved into winter. It was strange to go out into the street and find men there in the daytime. It had a feeling of fright in it, and always, the mood of the men grew uglier.

Of course, if they had so desired, the filmmakers could have gotten this information across in other ways, such as having one of the characters say to the other, "It's been twenty-two weeks now, hasn't it?" or by including shots of the men in the street acting ugly. But the narration is not awkward, and it ties the information back to the perceptions of little Huw.

Actually, the focalization in *How Green Was My Valley* is rather varied— Ford makes no particular use of shots from Huw's point of view—instead the image-maker moves the camera around at will. The camera and the voice-over have divided certain responsibilities between them: the voice-over gives us expository information and tells us about Huw's feelings, but never gives us interior views of other characters; it is up to the camera to reveal, for instance, Angharad's uncontrollable passion for Mr. Gruffydd, or Bess Morgan's torment at losing her sons (which must have been particularly affecting to World War II audiences). Since the film has so clearly established the voice-over's privilege and power, the camera's independence does not strike me as being in the least disruptive, even when it captures scenes, such as the love scenes between Angharad and Mr. Gruffydd, at which young Huw is not present. Interestingly enough, in the novel Llewellyn took great pains to justify these scenes by having Huw accidentally overhear these exchanges. With a certain noblesse oblige, the filmmakers ignore questions of probability and allow narrating Huw the typical powers of omniscient image-makers.

Any film can use voice-over to orient the spectators and to convey a sugary nostalgia; *How Green Was My Valley*'s special quality stems from the fact that its narrative structure is intimately connected to, if not responsible for, its theme: the power of memory (which is explictly linked to the power of God) to defeat death and loss. At the film's conclusion, Bess, Angharad, and Bronwyn wait anxiously on a bleak hillside (their heads covered by shawls) for news of Mr. Morgan's fate in the mine cave-in. Suddenly Bess says that she has felt her husband and Ivor "come to her" and tell her "of the glory they had seen." * The mine elevator rises to the surface, little Huw cradles his dead father in his lap, and the preacher, Mr. Gruffydd, stands over them with his

---

*While both film and novel display divided attitudes towards religion, this text definitely substantiates George Bluestone's thesis in *Novels into Film* (Berkeley: Univ. of California Press, 1957), pp. 34–45, that adaptations tone down novels' religious or social criticism and play up romantic elements. Compare Bess Morgan's comments in the novel when she learns of her husband's excruciating death:

arms outstretched in the shape of a cross. Over a close-up of Huw's face the voice-over speaks:

> Men like my father cannot die. They are with me still. Real in memory as they were in flesh. Loving and beloved forever. How green was my valley then.

As at the beginning when the picture flashed back to the unspoiled valley, the image cuts now from the sad and ugly scene at the mine entrance to a montage of shots from happier days: the whole family eating supper, Bron's first arrival, Huw and Mr. Gruffydd gathering daffodils, Angharad walking through a gate. The final shots are especially memorable: first, Huw walking with his father on the crest of a hill; secondly, a shot of his five brothers all reunited on the crest of another hill; third, a rhyming return to Huw and his father. What is noteworthy here is the placement of the horizon—at least three-fourths of each frame is sky and the figures are suspended in fluffy clouds as if in heaven, an impression bolstered by the heavenly music and ringing of church

---

"God could have had him a hundred ways," she said, and tears burning white in her eyes, "but He had to have him like that. A beetle under the foot."

"He went easy, Mama," I said.

"Yes," she said, and laughed without a smile. "I saw him. Easy, indeed. Beautiful, he was, and ready to come before the Glory. . . . If I set foot in Chapel again, it will be in my box, and knowing nothing of it. O, Gwil, Gwil, there is empty I am without you, my little one." (Richard Llewellyn, *How Green Was My Valley* [New York: Macmillan, 1940], pp. 492–93)

bells. As Henderson also notes, the conclusion of the film never returns to narrating-now in the spoiled valley, but loops back again in time, or rather loops back, out of time. "Loving and beloved forever," little Huw, his family, and his green valley live forever both in the glory of God and the glory of the narrator's memory. And Ford's film graphically illustrates both the power of memory and the power of art, because Huw's family lives not only for him, but for the audience too. As long as the film endures, his family is immortal.

For many reasons then, it is impossible to imagine what this film would have been without voice-over. But perhaps the single most important effect of the technique is the relationship it creates between that voice and the viewer, a relationship not really comparable to that between the novel's narrator and the reader. For we actually hear this voice, the voice of a mature man, generally soft and reflective, but at times tinged with hardly restrained emotion. He speaks to us in an English refreshingly flavored with a (pseudo-) Welsh accent (Pichel is American) and idiomatic expressions. We build up a relationship with him; he is our friend, our guide, our storyteller; we look at little Huw with different eyes, knowing how he will grow up. And as viewers we feel that our presence is not only implicitly acknowledged by the film, but that we are vital to this narrator. In telling us about his past he relieves his loneliness and pain, and through our attention and sympathy his valley blooms again.

Foregrounding the Act of Storytelling and *All About Eve*

How Green Was My Valley is told from a vantage point of such knowledge and maturity and the correspondence between the voice-over and the image-maker is so close that we probably never consider questioning the narrative perspective. But if many films use voice-over to escape into the past, others use the technique to stress the fact that stories depend upon who tells them, or, as Walter Benjamin once put it: "Traces of the storyteller cling to the story the way the handprints of the potter cling to the clay vessel." [28]

Voice-over is a prime means of making viewers aware of the subjectivity of perception (focalization) and storytelling (narration). One common strategy to accomplish this aim is to have the narrator be in the story, but not central to it, as a "narrator-witness." This *Great Gatsby*–syndrome appears not only in the two adaptations of that novel, but also in *The Power and the Glory,* King Vidor's *Ruby Gentry* (1952), and Alan Pakula's *Sophie's Choice* (1982), films where a friend of the central character narrates, and viewers are forced to see the great man or woman as the witness sees him or her. The protagonist thus becomes something of an enigma, and we learn only what the witness learns. A second method is that of *Citizen Kane* and *Rashomon* (both of which, inci-dentally, contrary to common recollection, dive directly into flashbacks and use only the barest snippets of voice-over), namely, presenting the same story from several different narrating characters' points of view, thus encouraging the viewer to compare the narrators' slants and to work at building a composite.

By the same token, a film can create a contrast between the story of an embedded character-narrator and that of the image-maker. When we see the narrator narrating, and understand his or her motivations for doing so, we have more information pertinent to judging the story, and we have the "objective" frame provided by the image-maker to measure it against.

Film noir uses so much narration, and in so many different ways, that generalizations are risky. (The prototypical conception of a *noir* narrator is best embodied by Philip Marlowe or some other equally hard-boiled protagonist, but a goodly number of *noirs* actually use third-person narration, and others use witness-narrators.) One can note, however, that a large number of *noirs* use voice-over precisely to stress the narrative's subjective source. Nostalgia per se is not an element of *Double Indemnity, The Postman Always Rings Twice, Mildred Pierce, Dead Reckoning, The Lady from Shanghai,* or *Blade Runner;* these narrators don't want to return to the past, they want to know— and often are being compelled to explain—how "all this" came to pass. The time between narrating-now and story-now is much shorter (a few present strange amalgams of present-tense interior monologue and past-tense narration), and the narration generally catches up to the time of the discourse. Their stories, which have to do with crime and adultery, are almost always confessions and often these confessions revolve around problems of seeing and perceiving—they have been too trusting or too suspicious—they have misjudged themselves and the lay of the land. These narrators' stories climax in their recognition of their mistakes and their new ability to tell us what really happened.[29]

This brings us to an important point about all homodiegetic voice-over—it serves as a means of winning the viewer's understanding and identification. *Noirs* and the so-called women's films of the same time period present characters who are, for the most part, isolated from their society and their loved ones, suffering, and forced to make moral choices. By offering their stories in their own words, their narration enables them to earn our sympathy. In *Brief Encounter* Laura cannot talk to anyone about the anguish she feels at parting from Alex, so the film has her tell us. Similarly, Philip Marlowe and all the rest of his ilk are too hard-boiled to tell anybody anything personal—but through their narration the audience is uniquely privileged with glimpses of their real feelings.

Crossfire (Dmytryk, 1947), *The Locket* (Brahm, 1946), and *Passage to Marseilles* (Curtiz, 1944) are *noirs* with intricate narrative structures—flashbacks-within-flashbacks-within-flashbacks—demonstrating the degree to which Hollywood has toyed with narrative perspective. Though not a *noir, All About Eve* provides a richer example of the same phenomenon. Its structure is both original and highly convoluted: although Mankiewicz took the general plot outline and several characters from a short story in *Cosmopolitan,* Mary Orr's "The Wisdom of Eve," [30] there was no reason why he should have stuck to its narrative structure, and he didn't. Screenwriter-director Mankiewicz's approach differed from Ford's and resembled instead those of Welles and Huston: he once said that he wrote "essentially for audiences who come to listen to a film as well as to look at it," [31] and his scripts are (in)famous for the amount of dialogue they contain.

All About Eve is about failures of perception and misplaced trust. It centers on a small circle of theater people and illustrates the disruption caused by the ambition of a talented, but duplicitous, young actress, Eve Harrington (Anne Baxter). Margo Channing (Bette Davis), an older, established actress, takes Eve under her wing, but Eve betrays her both professionally and personally— even trying to steal away her lover, director Bill Samspon (Gary Merrill). Karen Richards (Celeste Holm), who is Margo's best friend, initially sympathizes with and aids the ingenue, but Eve repays her kindness by captivating her husband, Lloyd Richards (Hugh Marlowe), the most successful playwright in town. Watching Eve's progress from the outskirts of this circle, is Addison DeWitt (George Sanders), a renowned theater critic whose character Mankiewicz based partly on George Jean Nathan and partly on himself.

In *More About All About Eve,* Gary Carey notes that Mankiewicz decided to use multiple narrators "to create a composite portrait of Eve, as seen from three different points of view—those of Addison, Karen, and Margo. . . . The total effect was to be, according to Mankiewicz: 'a composite mosaic-like structure in which several characters, while narrating their remembrances of still another, construct not only a portrait of the character in question, but inadvertent self-portraits as well.'" Moreover, Mankiewicz determined that the last section of the film would not be mediated by a character-narrator, so that after getting several characters' versions of Eve, the audience would see her directly. [32]

More than anything else, studying voice-over prompts one to pause over beginnings. The film opens with a close-up of a gold award statuette on a pedestal surrounded by flowers. We hear a cultured male voice:

The Sarah Siddons Award for Distinguished Achievement is perhaps unknown to you. It has been spared the sensational and commercial publicity that attends such questionable honors as the Pulitzer Prize, and those awards presented annually by that film society. [33]

Now the camera pulls back and frames an elderly man speaking as he stands at a long table; it keeps slowly craning back and upwards, until the whole banquet room is revealed. The voice continues:

The distinguished looking gentleman is an extremely old actor. Being an old actor he will go on speaking for some time—it is not important that you hear what he says.

(And in fact, one realizes here, that although one sees the actor's lips moving, there is no synchronous sound, just music and the narrating voice.)

However, it is important that you know where you are and why you are here. This is the dining hall of the Sarah Siddons' Society. The occasion is its annual banquet and presentation of the highest honor our theater knows—the Sarah Siddons Award for Distinguished Achievement.

The voice tells us more about the occasion over shots of the banquet hall. Then, returning to a shot of the award arrangement:

The minor awards, as you can see, have already been presented. Minor awards are for such as the writer [mid-shot of Lloyd Richards] and director— since their function [mid-shot of Bill Sampson] is to construct a tower so that the world can applaud a light which flashes on top of it [return to shot of award arrangement, the camera dollies in on the gold statuette], and no brighter light has ever dazzled the eye than Eve Harrington. Eve. But more of Eve later. All about Eve, in fact.

The first thing one notices is that the voice here is actually in complete control of the image: the camera illustrates the information that the speaker provides, successively changing its position to match the content of the voice-over. This narrator is also in charge of the sound track, tuning out dialogue he decides we do not need to hear. Moreover, this voice addresses us explictly and welcomes us to the scene transpiring before him—note his use of the

present tense. He even claims responsibility for the film as a whole by providing an abstract and promising to tell us "all about Eve."

Having established its authority, this voice introduces himself in the next shot. The camera focuses on a middle-aged man, fastidiously dressed, smoking with a cigarette holder. His glance is practically straight at the lens.

> To those of you who do not read, attend the theater, listen to unsponsored radio programs or know anything of the world in which you live, it is perhaps necessary to introduce myself. My name is Addison DeWitt. My native habitat is the theater. In it I toil not, neither do I spin. I am a critic and commentator. I am essential to the theater.

Such an explicit introduction is rare in voice-over films, and the combination of Addison's gaze at the camera and his inference of the viewer's ignorance almost amounts to a challenge. Addison then goes on to introduce us to Karen Richards, Lloyd Richards, Max Fabian, and Margo Channing, offering background information and his personal assessment of each. The camera provides shots of each character as he discusses him or her, but not from Addison's physical point of view.

After these introductions, Addison notes that the chairman of the society "has finally arrived at our reason for being here." Now he allows synchronous sound to fade in and we hear the end of the presentation speech. The camera alternately presents shots of the chairman, of Addison looking sardonic and glancing thoughtfully towards Karen and Margo, and of the two women's reactions to praise of Eve's humility and devotion. (One notes here one shot that is so unusual it doesn't seem to have been authorized by Addison, but rather by the image-maker: the chairman refers to the award passing from his aged hands to Eve's young and lovely hands—cut to a high-angle close-up of soft, white hands resting quietly on a table.)

The chairman finishes speaking and Eve rises and comes towards the podium. The audience is clapping lustily. Addison's glances still fluctuate between the podium and Karen and Margo (who are not applauding). Eve reaches out for the award—but just as she is about to touch it Addison freezes the frame, synchronous sound stops, and the voice-over comes back in (ellipses denote pauses):

Eve. Eve, the Golden Girl. The cover girl, the girl next door, the girl on the moon . . . *Time* has been good to Eve. *Life* goes where she goes—she's been profiled, covered, revealed, reported, what she eats and what she wears and who she knows and where she was and when and where she's going . . . Eve . . . You all know all about Eve. . . .

What can there be to know that you don't know?

At this moment Addison looks towards Karen once more, and we cut to a close-up of Karen's face as she gazes at the podium. As if in answer to Addison's question, the camera dollies in on Karen, the picture starts to dissolve, and we hear Karen in voice-over:

When was it? How long? . . . It's June now. That was—early October, only last October. It was a drizzly night. I remember I asked the taxi to wait.

Mankiewicz now commences Karen's flashback of her first meeting with Eve.

My purpose in detailing the opening scene is to demonstrate that although Mankiewicz uses three character-narrators, they are not of equal status. Addison is the most powerful; he addresses us directly, provides necessary information, controls the camera and sound, and claims responsibility for the film. Furthermore, Addison elicits Karen's story; it is as if Karen begins to tell what she knows about Eve in answer to his unspoken command to reveal her secrets. In *More About All About Eve,* Carey informs us that Mankiewicz's original shooting script included many returns to the place and time of narrating, the banquet, which allowed each of the narrators to relinquish his or her story while the next character picked up the baton. But the film was overly long, so Twentieth Century–Fox cut out both the bridging sequences and the repetition of a crucial scene from two narrators' points of view.* The missing transitions create a problem later, because although we see and hear Karen begin to narrate, when Margo's voice abruptly comes in, we have no information about her epic situation: we can only guess that she, too, is narrating from the banquet table in response to Addison's curiosity. Nevertheless, because Addison is featured so prominently at the film's start, and their narration chimes in later, we temporarily decide that he serves as the frame narrator, and that both Karen and Margo act as embedded narrators.

In the flashback portion of the film as we have it, Mankiewicz moves from one narrator to another fairly frequently. The flashback breaks down into six sections:

1. Narrator: Karen
   Karen's first meeting with Eve and her introduction of Eve to her idol, Margo.
2. Narrator: Margo
   Margo takes Eve in as her secretary, but starts to doubt her loyalty. Bill's disastrous welcome-home party.
3. Narrator: Karen
   Karen plays a trick on Margo to make her late for the theater so that Eve, her understudy, will get a chance to perform.
4. Narrator: Addison
   Addison, invited by Eve to this performance, visits backstage afterwards, witnessing her attempt to seduce Bill Sampson.
5. Narrator: Karen
   Addison writes an article in which Eve is quoted disparaging Margo. Bill and Margo reconcile and get engaged. Eve blackmails Karen into

---

*Mankiewicz uses exactly this baton-passing structure in *The Barefoot Contessa* (1954), where the numerous narrators reflect on the heroine at her funeral. The scenes recording the transitions from one narrator to the next are so languid here that one suspects that *All About Eve* benefits from their absence. Studio dictatorship had its good points.

giving her the leading role in Lloyd's next play. The rehearsals are stormy; Karen knows that Lloyd is in love with Eve.

6. Narrator: Addison
   Out-of-town opening of new play. Addison's confrontation with Eve. Her brilliance in that play, the part for which she is receiving the Sarah Siddons Award.

Within each of these sections, the narrators speak in voice-over only intermittently, but the action is centered on the narrating character to the extent that the camera constricts itself to following the designated narrator's experiences. The narrator is present in every scene of his or her section, and thus we learn what the narrator learns about Eve. (Actually, there is a lapse during the party scene when the camera leaves Margo to record a private scene between Karen and Eve, but we know from Carey that this is the sequence the studio re-edited.) However, the scenic presentation is not focalized *through* the characters in the sense of including unusual numbers of point-of-view shots: the camera behaves as if the stories were being presented by a typical filmic image-maker.

Mankiewicz stresses that each of his narrators inadvertently paints a self-portrait. Most of this portraiture stems from our attention being concentrated upon the narrating character and his or her experiences with Eve. Margo emerges as self-pitying and self-indulgent, but generous, open, and direct; it is not insignificant that she, the great actress, is the first to see through Eve's performance. Karen displays her tender heart, but also naiveté and a certain cattiness. In each section, the voice-over encourages us to understand and empathize with the women's problems and isolation: Margo's justified suspicions of Eve when everyone thinks she's paranoid; Karen's guilt at her deception of Margo, and her baffled misery at Lloyd's fascination with Eve: "I felt helpless, that helplessness you feel when you have no talent to offer—outside of loving your husband. How could I compete? Everything Lloyd loved about me, he had gotten used to long ago." As mentioned above, revelations like these are the reason we think of first-person narration (in any medium) as leading to our identification with the character-narrator—the technique allows us access to thoughts and emotions the character wouldn't express out loud. It offers us a more intimate knowledge of these characters than we enjoy with any but our closest friends or family.

As for Addison, who speaks the most in voice-over, the quotes from the opening scene give a sample of how he reveals his wit and intelligence through his narration; unfortunately, print cannot duplicate his distinctive tone and inflections. But the full portrait of his personality takes longer to develop. At the film's beginning, we notice the sharp edge of his tongue, but he is our guide, our storyteller, and we are flattered to have a host of such standing and sophistication. He may have an acerbic streak, but we feel sure that this streak will be used for a noble purpose—in this case, to expose Eve's machinations. As the movie progresses, however, we see him escorting the voluptuous Miss Casewell (Marilyn Monroe) and urging her to practice her wiles on Max Fabian. We hear Lloyd and Bill, respectively, call him a "venomous fishwife" and a "professional manure-slinger"; we watch with fascination his calculated involvement with Eve.

At the film's climax, it is Addison—not Eve—who reveals his true colors to the audience; we already know how corrupt Eve is, but we may have been cherishing illusions about him. The moment comes when Eve tells him about her plans to take Lloyd from Karen and marry America's most successful playwright. Eve prods, "Well, say something—anything! Congratulations, skoal—good work, Eve!" There is a long pause while Addison angrily rises to his feet and then snarls, "What do you take me for?" Here we expect him to drop his cynical veneer and object to her moral bankruptcy—we expect him to prove that he has been worthy of the trust we have lodged in him implicitly. Instead, Addison's anger turns out to be motivated by Eve's presumption that she was free to sleep with anyone but him. He tells her:

> I am Addison DeWitt. I am nobody's fool, least of all yours. . . . I have not come to New Haven to see the play, discuss your dreams, or to pull the ivy from the walls of Yale! I have come to tell you that you will not marry Lloyd—or anyone else—because I will not permit it. . . . Because after tonight, you belong to me.

He has uncovered all of Eve's deceptions not to expose or thwart her, but to blackmail her into becoming his sexual possession. Eve remarks that his demands upon her sound medieval, like something out of an old melodrama; to be more precise, Addison (the venomous adder), is playing Mephistopheles come to claim a soul who has bitten too deeply into forbidden fruit.*

So our primary narrator is ultimately quite compromised, even though, like Milton's Satan, he remains devilishly attractive. If we allow this to sink in, then perhaps we realize that we, too, have been poor judges of character; we, too, have allowed flattery (the flattery of having such an intelligent guide amuse us with his witticisms) to cloud our perception. Perhaps we now experience a wisp of doubt as to whether the story just witnessed was told reliably, or whether it is just another example of Addison's professional mud-slinging. Mankiewicz doesn't really exploit the possibilities of unreliable narration; but, significantly, once Addison concludes this section, the director switches narrative agents.

---

*As this reading implies, on my first viewing, I was decidedly misled by Addison's characterization up until this revelation. However, I wonder if 1950 audiences, more familiar with Sanders' screen image, would have been more suspicious, for in the thirties and forties Sanders had alternated between leading-man roles and portrayals of polished cads, as in *Rebecca* and *The Ghost and Mrs. Muir*. Which only goes to illustrate, of course, the critical truism that interpretations depend not only on what is in the text itself, but also on the background and milieu of the "reader."

Addison's voice remarks that Eve was a great success in her opening night, and with his words we are returned to the freeze-frame at the banquet. The viewer then realizes that all of the long flashback has been told to us while narrating time was magically frozen. Mankiewicz once remarked that the reason he favored flashbacks was that they summon up "not only the effect of the past upon the present, but also the degree to which the past *exists* in the present." [34] The structure of *All About Eve* implies that all the events of the past year inform a split second of the award presentation.

Once the frame unthaws, however, the remainder of the film unrolls without voice-over, without a character as mediator. The structure is analogous to that of other films, such as Tay Garnett's *The Postman Always Rings Twice* (1946), which not only catch up to their narrating-now but outstrip it, surprisingly revealing that we have been mistaken all along—the voice we took to be the presenter of the primary diegesis is itself embedded in the image-maker's discourse. In *All About Eve* the third-person epilogue shows Eve returning to her hotel, too tired to attend the party in her honor; she discovers another ingenue waiting there, a young girl who will do unto Eve what Eve has done unto Margo. The epilogue shows us how weary and lonely Eve is, how empty of meaning the award is to her. Our new perspective allows us, for the first time, a drop of compassion for Eve: the image-maker, not Addison, finally tells us *all*.

From stressing that everyone has his or her own version of a story and that all perception is colored by the perceiver, it is only one small step to the creation of limited, deluded, or lying narrators and the inimitable chills of unreliable narration. Before we take that step, however, we must look at the other major category of voice-over narrators.

4

Third-Person Narrators

Fiction films with third-person voice-over narrators are decidedly less common than those using first person. One reason for this imbalance is that adaptations of novels with heterodiegetic narration are less likely to use voice-over; a film of *Jane Eyre* without Jane's narration is unthinkable, because the narrative is filtered through her consciousness, but *Pride and Prejudice* could be produced without voice-over (Leonard, 1940). We miss the prose and "tone of voice" of Austen's anonymous narrator, but the filmmakers partially compensate through the acting, the action, and the mise-en-scène. Thus, while from the late 1930s to the present the great majority of films made from novels with character-narrators use voice-over, the list of works written in the third-person that have been adapted *without* narration stretches on and on.

Furthermore, filmmakers sometimes supply heterodiegetic narration through printed titles rather than by using a voice. Such titles impart expositional information quickly, easily, quietly; they provide a mini-history lesson in David O. Selznick's *Gone with the Wind* (Fleming, 1939), precisely orient us in time and space in *Psycho* (Hitchcock, 1960), identify the characters of *Mean Streets* (Scorsese, 1973), and create an appropriate long, long ago, and far, far away atmosphere for *Star Wars* (Lucas, 1977). Titles are never truly neutral, their language and typography always serve to characterize the films' image-makers to some extent, but often filmmakers prefer the relative impersonality and authority of titles to more noticeable oral narration. Titles may even be used in conjunction with first-person voice-over; the image-maker of *Letter from an Unknown Woman* communicates with the audience via an expositional title, and it is only later that Lisa's embedded narration comes in.

"Cultured," "graceful" image-maker of *Letter from an Unknown Woman* sets the scene with a printed title.

Those fiction films that do use third-person voice-over tend to fall into one of three categories. The first, and smallest, consists of adaptations of novels with indispensable narrators. The narrator of Henry Fielding's *Tom Jones* impresses a reader as being just as crucial as Tom or Sophia, if not more so: in many ways he is more fully drawn and more realistic. In their adaptation, the director, Tony Richardson, and the script-writer, John Osborne, use Michael MacLiammoir's voice to duplicate the educated and ironical tone of the novel.

The second category is a cluster of epics, Westerns, and fantasies. In these genres filmmakers need to impart a great deal of expositional information or unify a story that ranges widely in time and space; narration accomplishes both tasks effortlessly. Furthermore, precisely because it is oral, voice-over can remind viewers of traditional storytellers, and so evoke the proper atmosphere for the legendary or pseudo-legendary subject matter. King Vidor's *Duel in the Sun* (1947), for instance, opens with shots of a sunset-drenched rock landscape, while a voice says:

> Deep among the lonely sun-baked hills of Texas, the weather-beaten stone still stands. The Comanches called it Squaw's Head Rock. Time cannot change its impassive face, nor dim the legend of the wild young lovers who found heaven and hell in the shadows of the rock. . . .

Such an opening, intoned by Orson Welles, stresses the gap in time between discourse and story and instantly gives legendary stature to the story that follows.

The third category is made up of films that purposely use narration to imitate documentaries or newsreels. War films and semi-documentaries rely on the voice not only for expository information but also for documentary authenticity and authority.

In all cases, one finds that the voice-over highlights the source of the narrative. Instead of the discourse seeming like a translucent pane of glass, such narration makes us aware of the pane's tint, thickness, and scratches.

Who Really Narrates?

Like character-narrators, heterodiegetic voice-over narrators speak only intermittently and do not mediate every moment of the story. Such narrators, along with the accompanying scenic presentation, are actually transmitted by the narrative agency I call the image-maker.

However, in terms of the viewer's relationship with this narrator, his or her belief in the narrator's prowess, the move from first person to third can be quite significant. By being heterodiegetic, such narrators are already set apart from the characters and the diegesis. Like an image-maker, they are unconstrained by our questioning their right or power to know so much. Furthermore, because, like image-makers, heterodiegetic narrators are also usually (though not always) frame narrators, they remain unseen, unearthly, throughout the text. Thus, it is often particularly easy to accept these voices at face value. We experience a kind of merging together of narrator and image-maker, so that the voice ultimately becomes for us the voice of the image-maker.[1] In *Apocalypse Now* we are asked to believe that Captain Willard (Martin Sheen) is the creator/mediator of the phantasmagorical events displayed before us; in *The Red Badge of Courage* we are asked to believe that the image-maker sounds exactly like James Whitmore. The latter requires a smaller leap of faith.

Notwithstanding the relative ease of believing in these invisible storytellers, there are a significant number of films in which one is tripped up in mid leap and made conscious of a disparity between the purported narrator and the sense of an image-maker who is genuinely in charge. In other words, the distance between the narrator and the image-maker can be large or virtually nonexistent. At the narrator's closest approach, the voice becomes the image-maker's mouthpiece, while at his furthest remove, the narrator is shown up as just another facet of the text created by the image-maker for his or her own reasons.

The factors determining the size of this gap are identical to those determining our degree of acceptance of the homodiegetic narrator's narrative stance.

These include the establishment of the connection between the voice and the story, the frequency of the narration, and the correspondence between the narrator's tone and words and what we see and hear.

Our sense of the voice's connection to the story usually comes just from the fact that it immediately provides us with an abstract or orientation. At the beginning of Sydney Pollack's *Jeremiah Johnson* (1972), while the camera shows Robert Redford getting off a boat at a trading village, a voice tells us:

> His name was Jeremiah Johnson and they say he wanted to be a mountain man. Story goes that he was a man of proper wit and adventurous spirit suited to the mountains. Nobody knows whereabouts he came from but [it] don't seem to matter much. . . . This here's his story.

"This here's his story" forges a link between "this here," the film we are watching, and this voice, a voice that sounds like an old-timer spinning yarns around a campfire. Although the voice never returns, we accept the rest of the film as the story he started to narrate orally. If you listen carefully, you will find that numerous third-person films begin with phrases like "my story," "our story," "our hero," "this is the story," or "here is the story"; such possessive pronouns and demonstrative adjectives cement the connection between the off-screen speaker and the unfolding drama. A maxim should be engraved: "He who provides an abstract of the story to come, 'owns' that story."

The frequency of the voice's commentary is not in itself a determining factor, but one that can weigh in the balance. The more he speaks, the more the film's discourse appears consistent, and the more we can judge how well the narrator's comments correspond to the scenic presentation.

The correspondence between the tone and content of the narration and the images and action once again brings up the question of point of view. Usually the verbal narration "fits" with the picture track and with the mood of the text as a whole, yet in some cases we note large disparities. Such is true of the beginning of George Stevens' *The More the Merrier* (1943), where a corny voice starts talking about how cultured, polite, and hospitable Washington, D.C., is, while the screen shows overcrowded cabs, fast-food counters, and No Vacancy signs. The viewer soon realizes that the voice can hardly be in charge, but rather that, for reasons of his own, the image-maker has chosen to start the film with a parody of travelogues.

Interestingly enough, the casting of the narrator and the viewer's knowledge about this casting also influence perceptions of the voice-over's role. Filmmakers strive to find exactly the right voice quality, accent, and inflections for their subject matter. (The tip-off that a narrator is being satirized is often his exaggeratedly smug or pompous tone.) Moreover, filmmakers use casting to play upon the viewer's knowledge of other texts. Cy Enfield's *Zulu* (1964), for instance, uses Richard Burton, "the once and future king," to narrate a story about the massacre of British troops; Mel Brooks uses Orson Welles's narration in his parody of movie epics, *History of the World, Part I* (1981).

Yet older fiction films (and some from more recent years) nearly always omitted giving the narrator screen credit. None of the explanations for this omission I have heard—namely, that actors considered narrating low in prestige and were not eager for credit; that since voice-over was generally the last thing added, the credits had already been made up; or that in the early years the studios were chary about awarding credits in general—are quite satisfactory. Whatever the actual reasons behind the policy—which, by the way, also holds true for first-person films that use a separate actor as narrating-I (Irving Pichel gets no screen credit for *How Green Was My Valley,* neither does Kim Stanley for *To Kill a Mockingbird*)—the anonymity of the narrator makes him or her even more mysterious and even less human, and thus aids our association of the voice and the image-maker.

Frequently filmmakers cast themselves. We all know that Welles has narrated his own films, but so have John Huston, Carol Reed, Cecil B. De Mille, Jean Cocteau, François Truffaut, and Jean-Luc Godard. Directors rarely give themselves a narration credit and viewers must either recognize their voices or learn about their roles from outside sources. But if the viewer is privy to this information, he or she closes the gap between the image-maker and the narrating voice with a resounding thud, since on a practical, if not theoretical, level, the voice does belong to the maker of the images.

The Circumstances of Narration

Contrary to popular belief, not all third-person narrators are frame narrators. The fact that such narrators are relatively rarely embedded does not make embedding impossible on formal grounds. Whenever a character launches into a story in which he or she does not participate, that character, like Scheherazade, is an embedded heterodiegetic narrator. Neither Genette nor any of his recent followers have clearly delineated what it means "to participate" or "not to participate" in a story; I think the issue hinges not upon whether the narrator is telling a story "about himself" but on whether he or she exists in the same fictive world as the characters, whether he or she could possibly know them and they know him or her. Thus, embedded heterodiegetic voice-over narrators relate stories that are far removed in time: for example, the priest in *Forgotten Commandments* recounts a Bible story, and the old hermit in Hal Roach's *One Million B.C.* (1940) talks about prehistory. In other cases the narrator's tale is heterogeneous because its status as *fiction* is stressed; for example, in Vincente Minnelli's *Madame Bovary* (1949), Gustave Flaubert (James Mason) narrates Emma's life story while he is on the witness stand defending himself against the obscenity charges brought against the novel. In such films the narrators are embedded because we see them in the act of narrating—because they are thus placed within the image-maker's discourse—yet they tell stories in which they play no role. Perhaps the most frequent examples of such narrators are those television hosts who both introduce the story on-screen and provide voice-over, such as Rod Serling in "Twilight Zone."

In the above cases, we know that these narrators are embedded because we see them in the act of narrating. Even though we never see anyone narrating *News on the March* in *Citizen Kane*, we also have no trouble classifying that voice as a micro-narrator, because the newsreel is presented as a discrete, isolated text. But Ingmar Bergman's *Cries and Whispers* (1972) is puzzling and disturbing: it has been running some ten or fifteen minutes before an anonymous voice breaks in with narration. It is difficult to accept this tardy speaker as the teller of a film that has already been unfolding for quite a while, so even though this voice is not obviously diegetic, I think of him not as teller, but as told, perhaps a parody of typical narrators' certainties, part of the whispering torment of the three sisters. As we found in chapter 3, in order to accept the voice-over as primary, as the teller of the whole film, the voice must speak at the very beginning.

Since the overwhelming majority of third-person narrators are frame narrators, let us here concentrate on analyzing their epic situations. These situations are nebulous, but rather than throw up our hands, we might endeavor to understand how this ambiguity affects our viewing experience. Critics commonly categorize such narrators as speaking from "nowhere" and drop the subject. Yet, as Noël Burch points out, "Off-screen sound . . . *always* brings off-screen space into play." [2] Hence, the addition of extradiegetic sound forces the viewer to realize that the story is itself framed by other space and other time, that the "world" pictured on the screen is enveloped by another world of discourse-here and discourse-now. In short, the addition of oral narration again directs our attention to the double-layering of story and discourse. (The same is true of novels with third-person narrators, but such double-layering may have less impact there, because the events and the narration are both conveyed verbally.) We may have no information about the narrator's world, because we never see it, but it affects our experience of the narrative. Theoretically, there is no reason why a frame narrator should not tell us something about his world, or why moviemakers should not, by imaginative use of sound effects, convey more color than is typically evoked by taping narration in sound-proof booths. Television commercials occasionally demonstrate creative manipulation of the sound of the narration track.

From what point in time does the narrator narrate? Franz Stanzel has noticed that in literature the omniscient third-person narrator "is usually content with a more or less vague indication of his posteriority to the narrated material. . . . Moreover, the authorial narrator in no way feels himself permanently committed to some initially specified temporal distance from the narrated events. Frequently he moves right up to the scene."[3] Stanzel's observations apply neatly to voice-over films: usually the entire story is recounted in the past tense and the impression is given that the narration postdates the events on the screen. On the other hand, Lubitsch's *To Be or Not to Be* provides an example of extreme slipperiness. It starts in the present: over shots of a busy street scene, we hear, "We're in Warsaw, the capital of Poland. It's August, 1939. . . ." Later, when story time has progressed past the September Nazi invasion, the narrator comes back in and surveys the destruction of the city: "A curtain *had fallen* on the Polish drama, a tragedy with no relief in sight. There *was* a Nazi tank against every Polish hope, and the people *were* stunned and helpless" (my emphasis). Thus, the narrator, who started speaking in August, is now tacitly claiming to be situated at some point later than September—he has not only kept up with the story, he has outdistanced it. Because they are never bound to human form, these narrators have even more leeway than character-narrators in shifting their epic situation without ruffling our suspension of disbelief.

To whom do these narrators address their stories? Since we are aware of no other listeners, we always assume that the narrator is talking to *us*. As mentioned earlier, this couches the film as a deliberate communication and allows for a certain intimacy between viewers and the narrating voice. Often filmmakers exploit this relationship by having the narrator explicitly and self-consciously address the audience. In Richard Quine's *The Solid Gold Cadillac* (1956), George Burns begins:

> Ladies and Gentlemen, in this country today, more people are investing in the stock market than ever before. I imagine some of you folks own stock in one company or another. . . .

Such direct address prompts an active involvement in the film—we tend to nod our heads and think about our meager or nonexistent portfolios.

Through what medium does the narrator narrate? The few films that do show us third-person narrators in the act demonstrate once again a propensity for *oral* epic situations. As for the frame narrators, since we never see them in the act, and they rarely give us any hints, we have very little information to go on. I believe, however, that because we hear the voice, we suppose that the narrator is presenting his story orally. This impression is bolstered by all those beginnings where the narrator refers to "my story," "our story," or "this story," when, after all, he could have said "this film."

One thing that film can do that literature cannot is to narrate via song. Many films make minimal use of this option by merely including an opening

Cat Ballou's troubadours

theme song that provides narrative information. However, at least two cases, Charles Walter's *High Society* (1956) and Elliot Silverstein's *Cat Ballou* (1965), pioneer a more thorough integration. In the former, Louis Armstrong, who figures as a character in the film, intermittently bursts into narrating song. In the latter, Nat King Cole and Stubby Kaye appear in the guise of strolling minstrels, yet one hardly knows whether to label them homodiegetic or heterodiegetic: we see them on the screen, but they are invisible to all the other characters and face the camera directly; some of their singing is done on camera and some in voice-over. Cole and Kaye turn the film into "The Ballad of Cat Ballou" and use the song both for expositional information, such as, "It was a hanging day in Wolf City, Wyoming . . . 1894"; and for commentary: "Cat Ballou, she's mean and evil through and through." Our experience of the film, naturally, is greatly affected not only by the narrators' words and voice qualities, but also by the lively melody and orchestration.

Omniscience

When no barriers keep us from accepting the heterodiegetic voice as the teller of the entire film, we almost always characterize him as "omniscient," but we rarely consider exactly what we mean by this term, or to what extent it truly applies.

Amalgamating the findings of theorists such as Abrams, Booth, Chatman, Genette, Scholes and Kellogg, and Stanzel, we learn that "omniscience" implies any or all of the following qualities:

1. Knowing much more than any of the characters in the story, or even, in Chatman's words, "Knowing All, where 'all' includes the outcome of every event and the nature of every existent." However, Chatman reminds us that "Knowing All, of course, need not mean Telling All."[4]
2. Freedom in space and time (called "multifariousness" by Scholes and Kellogg, "omnipresence" by Chatman); basically, the ability to intermix scenes of different locales, or centering upon different characters, regardless of the activities of any single character.
3. Privileged access to characters' thoughts and feelings: in general, the more characters a narrator can delve into, the more we perceive him to be omniscient.

How do these definitions mesh with film narrators? The know-it-all flavor of the narrator's commentary is largely responsible for our attribution of omniscience. Voice-over narrators are big on facts and figures, on historical data, on telling us all about the character's birth, family, or past—in short, on passing along information that can be transmitted visually or dramatically only with difficulty. But in addition to providing orientations, these narrators, who speak for (or rather *as*) the image-maker, are particularly likely to provide guidance concerning what conclusions the viewers should draw. They tend to voice the ideological and/or moral agenda behind the film. Taking advantage of their remove from the story, they are generally heavier on Labovian evaluation than first-person narrators, more likely to use their platform to probe, judge, generalize, and interpret.

As for spatial, temporal, or scenic flexibility, even without voice-over, films put Father Time through his paces, and nearly always demonstrate omnipresence, now showing us what is happening with one character, now following another on the other side of the room or country. Very, very rarely will a film such as *Lady of the Lake* stay tightly focalized through one character the way that Henry James's *The Ambassadors* is consistently focalized through Lambert Strether. The addition of third-person narration simply allows filmmakers to traverse continents or decades without fear of leaving the viewer behind. The overt presence of the narrator, who speaks from a privileged vantage point and knits together all the loose threads, allows for any number of shifts of focalization without strain.

However, the third aspect of literary omniscience, privileged access to a character's consciousness (focalization "from within"), does not apply to film. All the painstaking work in narrative theory measuring the distance between the narrative discourse and the character's consciousness in terms of syntax—that is, on the basis of whether a comment is "tagged" (assigned to a character with a "she said" or "he thought"), or "untagged," and whether it is "direct" (the character refers to himself as "I") or "indirect," (the narrator refers to the character as "he" or "she")—is largely irrelevant to narrative cinema. A film narrator is perfectly capable of telling us what characters are thinking, yet such "inside views" seldom occur. Traditionally, since film is not exclusively mediated through such a narrator, it has employed other means to reveal characters' thoughts and emotions, including nuances of performance, close-ups, expressionistic lighting, or music. When verbalization of inner states is desirable or necessary, films are more likely to allow characters to express themselves directly through interior monologue than to have the narrator articulate their feelings.

Our impression of third-person narrators' omniscience comes not only from the ways in which their methods tally with theoretical definitions but also from powerful stereotypes. *The March of Time* greatly influenced American perceptions of such speakers, and booming "voice of God" narrators, speaking with asinine assurance, have surrounded us in newsreels, documentaries, training films, and commercials ever since. Since the late 1950s many documentarians, particularly those on the left, have thought that all third-person narrators abuse their podiums, becoming elitist, oppressive spokesmen for the ruling class. Rejected by documentarians and critics alike as authoritarian and offensive, the technique has been in disfavor for two decades.

Critical opinion has just recently come to the conclusion that the avoidance of narration is no guarantee of egalitarianism or objectivity, that "showing" is really just another and more covert form of "telling," about which one might have more political or moral squeamishness. Mary Ann Doane, following Pascal Bonitzer,[5] believes that documentaries that eschew narration actually promote "the illusion that reality speaks and is not spoken, that the film is not a constructed discourse. In effecting an 'impression of knowledge,' a knowledge which is given and not produced, the film conceals its own work and posits itself as a voice without a subject. The voice is even more powerful in silence. The solution, then, is not to banish the voice but to construct *another* politics."[6] Bill Nichols, too, complains that "far too many contemporary film-makers appear to have lost their voice. . . . Formally, they disavow the complexities of voice, and discourse, for the apparent simplicities of faithful observation or respectful representation. . . . Very few seem prepared to admit through the very tissue and texture of their work that all film-making is a form of discourse fabricating its effects, impressions, and point of view."[7]

Bonitzer and Nichols both make concrete suggestions for returning to voice-over narration: Bonitzer believes that we can compromise the voice's inherent authority if we multiply or divide it, make it relate to the image-track obliquely or ironically, and/or if we give the podium to the sex heretofore virtually shut out from these roles—women. Nichols praises narration that is self-conscious and self-reflexive, that foregrounds instead of hides the role of the filmmaker(s) in the production of the discourse.

Taking a slightly different tack, Jeffrey Youdelman argues that the prejudices against narration have been based on less than complete information. "Progressive filmmakers have just reason to reject [voice of God] models," he states, "but they neither exhaust the vast possibilities for narration today nor represent the sum total of the past." [8] He goes on to discuss certain British and American documentaries of the 1930s and 1940s, films such as *Night Mail, The River,* and *Native Land* (Hurwitz and Strand, 1942), which use voices that are lyrical, passionate, and populist, rather than preachy, officious, or authoritarian.

In line with Youdelman's advice to reevaluate the past before making any theoretical pronouncements, I should like to take a long look at the particularly interesting use of third-person voice-over narration in *The Naked City.*

Humanizing the "Voice of God" and *The Naked City*

Fiction films actually have a long history of making fun of "voice of God" narration. From Michael Curtiz's *Casablanca* (1943) to Woody Allen's *Take the Money and Run* (1969) to Jamie Uys's *The Gods Must Be Crazy* (1980), directors have found documentary narrators an easy and tempting target. However, the majority of films that have imitated such narration have done so not in order to deflate documentary practices but to stress their stories' factual bases, and to borrow documentary authority to ennoble their fictions. *The Naked City* falls into this category.

The Naked City is probably the best-known example of the series of semi-documentaries produced in the late forties after the war ended and filmmakers who had been recruited or conscripted into government documentary production were demobilized. Their new familiarity with documentary techniques, coupled with the rising costs of Hollywood labor (particularly set building), the shortage of studio space,[9] and possibly a craving for dramas that reached beyond the confines of the sound studios (Italian neorealism flourished during the same time period), led to films such as Henry Hathaway's *House on 92nd Street* (1945) and *13 Rue Madeleine* (1946), Elia Kazan's *Boomerang* (1947), and Anthony Mann's *T-Men* (1948). For the most part these films based their plots on case histories and relied on location shooting; despite their holding on to rather conventional storylines and stock characters, these semi-documentaries were eager to assert their independence from the studio and to claim documentary credibility and authority. With notable exceptions, the cycle burned itself out in theatrical films in the 1950s, but was kept alive on television in "Gangbusters," "Naked City," "The Untouchables," and "The F.B.I." (That both "Gangbusters" and "Dragnet" originated as radio shows should alert us again to radio's underappreciated influence.)

In many ways *The Naked City* is prototypical: it was shot on 107 different locations in New York City, using authentic exteriors, apartments and offices, New Yorkers as extras, natural lighting, and a storyline that amalgamates several police case histories. The film follows the efforts of a pair of New York detectives, veteran Lieutenant Dan Muldoon (played by Barry Fitzgerald), and young Sergeant Jimmy Halloran (played by Don Taylor), to solve the murder of Jean Dexter, a model drowned in a bathtub. After laboriously tracking down numerous leads, the detectives uncover a stolen jewelry ring and elicit confessions from the major participants. They also close in on the murderer, but Willie Garzah (Ted de Corsia), eludes capture and leads them on a climactic chase over the Williamsburg Bridge, where the police eventually have to shoot him.

The other semi-documentaries use voice-of-God narrators, pontificating from on high; occasionally these narrators' pretensions are so extreme that they clash with the subtleties of the dramas. *The Naked City,* however, imitates the quieter, more lyrical style of the classic British documentaries, and then further defines and humanizes its disembodied voice to the point where, although the narrator remains off-screen, he becomes completely distinct and individual. Yet, paradoxically, the narrator of *The Naked City* gives up neither the film's claim to documentary authenticity nor his own omniscience, credibility, and flexibility.

Why did *The Naked City* end up with such unique narration? Its production history provides some clues, since it clearly illustrates the tug of numerous influences: wartime training film, classic documentary, poetry, literature, journalism, and the personalities of its creators.[10]

The film's story and the first draft of its screenplay were commissioned by Mark Hellinger from Malvin Wald, a screenwriter who had then just returned from several years of making wartime documentary and training films. Wald was responsible for urging the semi-documentary approach, for basing the plot on New York police cases, and for meticulously researching police procedures. While in the Army Motion Picture Unit, Wald had been exposed to, and impressed by, various classic documentaries, and he has singled out Walter Ruttmann's *Berlin, die Symphonie einer Grossstadt,* Lorentz's *The Plow That Broke the Plains,* and Van Dyke and Steiner's *The City* as particularly influencing his conception of this film. Furthermore, Wald has informed me that he ultimately conceived of the personality of the narrator as a combination of Walt Whitman and Thomas Wolfe, "A combination of poet-novelist (hence Whitman-Wolfe) portraying the multi-layered lifestyle . . . of a large city."

Wald's screenplay was rewritten by Albert Maltz, a playwright, short-story writer, novelist, and screenwriter of award-winning documentaries and fiction films. Maltz may have been responsible for sharpening the film's social commentary; for many years he was a Communist party member and later gained renown as one of the Hollywood Ten. The film was directed by Jules Dassin, the director of Hellinger's previous production, *Brute Force;* like Maltz, Dassin would later be blacklisted for his left-wing politics. Ultimately, however, Dassin did not have much control over *The Naked City.* He once told *Sight and Sound* that the film was edited over his objections, and that "When [he] saw *Naked City* for the first time, [he] could have wept." [11]

The final determining influence on the film as a whole, and on the narration in particular, was Mark Hellinger's. Hellinger, then an independent producer, had been a popular journalist, columnist, writer of short stories, plays, and screenplays (and also a notorious check-grabber, high-liver, and friend of mobsters), but up until then, according to Wald, he had never "seen or even cared to be associated with a documentary." Although Hellinger routinely collaborated on the screenplays he produced, he was originally nonplussed by Wald's semi-documentary approach. At some point, however, Hellinger decided to read the narration himself. This decision was certainly motivated by his belief that he could express his fascination with New York better than any actor he might hire, but one might also credit Hellinger's habitual hunger for the limelight. At any rate, Hellinger not only probably influenced Maltz's revisions, but also made further changes during post-production; I note numerous major discrepancies between the published Maltz-Wald shooting script of May 1947 and the finished film, and most of these enlarge and refine the narrator's role. Hellinger's personal influence on the film was so obvious to his contemporaries that Bosley Crowther wrote in his *New York Times* review, "the late Mark Hellinger's personal romance with the City of New York was one of the most ecstatic love affairs of the modern day . . . this picture . . . is a virtual Hellinger column on film." [12] (Hellinger died of a heart attack before the film was released. He was forty-four.)

Thus, the film's narrator was composed of a series of overlays: on the bottom, the documentary observer/investigator who is going to inform the viewer of police routine and present a picture of city life; on top of that, a less stiff Whitmanesque persona who wants to capture the soul of this city and demonstrate the excesses of its commercialism; on top of that, Mark Hellinger, the individual. But Hellinger's crucial casting decision led automatically to two more overlays: first, since he publicly identified himself so closely with New York (the publicity posters called him " 'Mr. New York' himself") the voice becomes the voice of The City; secondly, since Hellinger was the film's producer and thoroughly in charge at every step, there is no question but that this voice speaks as the film's image-maker.

All of the layers are immediately perceivable in the film's unusual opening, a sequence not in the published script.[13] The film starts with an aerial shot of lower Manhattan and we hear very muted propeller noise. As the shot moves northwards, an off-screen voice says:

Ladies and Gentlemen, the motion picture you are about to see is called *The Naked City.* My name is Mark Hellinger; I was in charge of its production. And I may as well tell you frankly that it's a bit different from most films you've ever seen. It was written by Albert Maltz and Malvin Wald, photographed by William Daniels, and directed by Jules Dassin.

As you can see, we're flying over an island, a city, a particular city, and this is the story of a number of its people, and the story, also, of the city itself. It was *not* photographed in a studio. Quite the contrary. Barry Fitzgerald, our star, Howard Duff, Dorothy Hart, Don Taylor, Ted de Corsia and the other actors played out their roles on the streets, in the apartment houses, in the skyscrapers, of New York itself. . . .

This is the city as it is, hot summer pavements, the children at play, the buildings in their naked stone, the people without makeup.

The narrator's claim that he knows and presents The Truth comes through very clearly in this opening—"This is the city *as it is,*" he says—and the camera offers a God's-eye view of the city, stretched out below, baring itself for his inspection. But this observer could hardly be more self-conscious, more self-reflexive—he introduces the crew and actors, he describes the circumstances of the film's production. He even, quite remarkably, refers to the film as a film. Through the airplane noise and through his admission, "We're flying over an island," he partially explains his epic situation and thus neutralizes the camera's privileged viewpoint. At the same time, the narration strives for a lyrical, Whitmanesque tenor, cataloguing the varied facets of the city: "hot summer pavements, the children at play, the buildings in their naked stone, the people without makeup." But this narration differs crucially from that of, say, Lorentz's *The River*, because the narrator does not pretend to speak for a corporate entity (Hellinger introduces himself forthrightly and keeps referring to himself as "I"), and because his informal diction and somewhat scratchy, nasal voice (suggesting a life of drinking and smoking), are the antithesis of professional narrators like Westbrook Van Voorhis or Thomas Chalmers. Throughout this opening, and indeed throughout the film, we never lose sight of the fact that our guide is a real person, the person responsible for the film.

Let us examine more closely some of this narrator's characteristics and strategies. As we have seen, this narrator gives up none of the typical documentary narrator's knowledge or power. Like a "voice of God" or "voice of history," he is omniscient. This narrator imparts background information about the characters' personal lives (for instance, he tells us about Halloran's previous police duty and war experiences), and provides data on city life and police procedures. Furthermore, he is prescient: he knows that the cleaning woman Martha Swenson is to find the body before she even enters Jean Dexter's apartment building.

Moreover, he evinces complete freedom in time and space, cutting around the metropolis at will. The narrator can be everywhere, virtually at once; an opening montage sequence presents the city at 1 A.M. on a hot summer night: Wall Street deserted, a bank closed, a factory idle, a ship at dock, a man sleeping restlessly, the elevated subway still running, a plane flying in. In addition, the film follows several characters' activities, switching back and forth between them as suits its fancy, rather than staying focalized through or on a single protagonist.

Furthermore, *The Naked City* apparently substantiates Bonitzer's claim that "the power of the voice is a stolen power, a usurpation." [14] Sometimes, especially during exterior scenes, when synchronous sound recording would have been too difficult, the narrator literally takes words out of characters' mouths and either summarizes their conversations in indirect discourse or speaks their dialogue himself. For example, when the cops are trying to find Garzah, we see shots of detectives approaching shopkeepers, but we do not hear them speak, instead the narrator speaks for them. (Although he sometimes speaks their dialogue for them, the narrator never overtly offers us inside views of characters' thoughts or feelings. It is up to the camera to focus on their expressions and gestures, up to the actors to find the right nuance.)

Narrator [voice-over]: For this woman, the day will not be ordinary.

Narrator [voice-over]: Lady, ever see a man looks like this?

Narrator [voice-over]: Mister, ever see a man looks like this?

On the other hand, this film also provides a case study of one of Bonitzer's suggestions for redistributing power—that is, multiplying the unseen voices, thereby creating a *Rashomon* effect, each voice commenting on the others: during the montage sequences, we swoop in and out of various "representative" New Yorkers' minds and hear their thoughts in voice-over interior monologue. Thus, for instance, near the film's beginning, we hear the thoughts of a woman mopping the floor of Radio City Music Hall, of a radio disc jockey, and of a young mother. These frequent interpolations onto the narration track seem to be designed to let other New Yorkers have their say and to break up the narrator's monopoly, encouraging viewers to consider the narrator's voice as just one among many. And yet, one cannot forget that the comments of these "New Yorkers" have been scripted for them, and that even if they were authentic, they only got on the track at all through the sufferance of the film-makers. There is no help for it: *The Naked City* offers this narrator's version of the story, and other versions—particularly Jean Dexter's—never get a hearing.

But what a distinctly individual version he offers! Although this narrator can be thought of as Knowing All, he certainly does not Tell All; he often feigns ignorance and teases us with bits of information that we will not be able to assimilate until later (or a second viewing). For example, in the film's second sequence, the narrator's seemingly random ruminations give characters

Woman [voice-over]: Sometimes I think the world is made up of nothing but dirty feet.

Man [voice-over]: You put on a record, you take it off. You put on another. Does any-one listen to this program except my wife?

Woman [voice-over]: Some babies are 8 o'clock babies; some babies are 7 o'clock babies, why do you have to be a 6 o'clock baby?

we don't even know yet alibis for a murder that has not yet been committed. In fact, this narrator's commentary is often quite oblique. Over shots of rush hour crowds on the street, ferry, and subway, he remarks:

> They're tired, they're hot, they're hungry, but they're on their way home. In the newspapers, there's a new murder story. It hit the headlines. Full layout and pictures on page 3. It's really quite sensational.

The narrator doesn't say anything about the tabloids providing the titillation and excitement that these tired working people crave to take their minds off their discomfort, doesn't say anything about how sad and exploitative it is that the public gets a thrill out of this young woman's death—he just puts a light stress on "sensational" and lets the word twist in the wind.

Additional aspects of the narration suggest that despite the narrator's knowledge and powers, he does not have a stranglehold on screen action. Significantly, he moves his epic situation as the film progresses, always using the present tense: "*It's* an hour later now, 6 A.M.," he says, or "*Now it's* time to go to work." Whereas a film such as *Duel in the Sun* stresses the distance in time between discourse and story to create nostalgia, this film creates synchronicity between discourse-now and story-now in order to create a sense of

Dr. Stoneman at a card party during the murder.
Narrator [voice-over]: And while some people work, others are rounding up an evening of relaxation.

Ruth and Niles at a nightclub during the murder.

Narrator [voice-over]: Hi ya, Halloran. Here's a question for you. How many jewelry shops in the city of New York? Be patient, you're about to find out.

Narrator [voice-over]: Hello, Constantino. A detective finds himself in odd places doesn't he? How about a mud pack, no? Well, how about a permanent? Or how about those eyebrows, ever have them plucked?

immediacy. Instead of events seeming unalterable, tidily contained by the past, or regurgitated with a biased slant, the story is unfolding *now,* and the narrator, like a radio sportscaster, is just looking on, calling the shots.

But perhaps the most unusual rhetorical strategy employed by the film is the narrator's habit of addressing comments *to the characters,* as if he were off to the side, watching every move they make and reacting with teasing, questions, or advice to which they are oblivious.* Hellinger uses this technique throughout the film, but it plays a particularly important role at the climax (another portion that departs from the published script). When Garzah knows that the police are after him, the camera shows him in long-shot, quickly walking down a crowded street. The narrator addresses him:

The cops are on a manhunt, Garzah. You need a plan; you've got to get out of this neighborhood. Stop to look at a tie; maybe you're being shadowed.

The next shot catches Garzah in the thick of a crowd at a bus stop.

You've got to get out of this neighborhood. That's it, a crowded bus is safer for you than a taxi.

The bus, too packed to accept more passengers, closes its doors and drives off.

Tough luck. But you can't wait for the next one. How about the subway?

*Similar apostrophes can be found in *A Letter to Three Wives,* where Addie Ross laughs wickedly at characters who are oblivious to her, and in John Sturges's *Old Man and the Sea,* where the heterodiegetic narrator tries to encourage the old man. Television commercials have pioneered a twist—allowing direct exchanges between anonymous announcers and on-screen characters, thus punching holes in the barriers that separate homodiegetic and heterodiegetic.

Garzah tries to cross a busy street, but his way is blocked by the traffic and by a traffic cop who glares at him. The narrator, sounding very excited, increases the tension:

>   Take it easy Garzah, don't run!

Garzah starts running up the steps to the Williamsburg Bridge.

Don't call attention to yourself!

Garzah runs into a blind man and his seeing-eye dog; the startled dog grabs his sleeve.

It's only an accident, Garzah, pass it off!

As we see Garzah reach for his gun, the narrator shouts at him:

Don't lose your head!! Don't lose your head!!!

The camera cuts away to show the police planning their encirclement; off-screen we hear a shot—Garzah *has* lost his head, he's shot the dog, and this noise ultimately leads to the police cornering him. The narrator's comments in this scene have kept us fully abreast of the racing of Garzah's mind, his one chance for escape and how he loses it. Furthermore, the couching of this information as conversation, rather than as authoritative commentary (such as, "Garzah, trapped like a rat, knew that he had to get out of that neighborhood"), increases our sense of the character's independence and reality. Finally, this strategy heightens our awareness of the narrator's humanity and stimulates our own reaction to these events. We have all been at films where someone from the audience has shouted "Don't go in there!" or "There's the shark!" at the screen, and often we have wanted to shout ourselves. Here the narrator acts as our surrogate—he is shouting at Garzah for *us*. Ultimately, then, the narrator becomes the voice of the viewer.

In fact, far from keeping an elitist distance from us, the narrator does everything possible to accentuate his connection with the viewers and to place himself on our level. He starts *The Naked City* by introducing himself, and as it progresses he continues to address us frequently and informally with wry comments. Instead of booming at us from on high, his diction and tone of voice are consistently natural: a friend of Hellinger's has testified that he speaks "just as he would to a crony down at Joe's Bar and Grill." [15] This narrator is not particularly wise; the *New Yorker* may be justified in complaining that "Mr. Hellinger's remarks are about as penetrating as the spiel of a guide on a sightseeing bus." [16] But by the film's end, we have a very clear sense of the narrator's personality—his self-aggrandizement, his cynicism, his sentimentality, his devotion to The City and its inhabitants. This narrator combines both authority and warmth: he is powerful yet fallible, the voice of New York and the voice of one man, part lecturer, part tour-guide, part barside raconteur. In short, he is a very human storyteller.

The Naked City provides an example of a film that doesn't fit the stereotype, where the narration is not only inoffensive, but creative and refreshing. Nor is *The Naked City* an isolated instance; other fiction films, such as *She Wore a Yellow Ribbon, The Solid Gold Cadillac,* and *Cannery Row* can be singled out for their narrators' relaxed tones and sense of humor. In fictional contexts, the temptation to sound like God has always had to compete with other models, such as the temptation to sound like a chatty bedtime storyteller. We should note that these films temper the narrator's authority not through any radical reworking of the form but through their scripts and casting. *The Naked City* uses some of the rhetorical strategies recently suggested by critics, such as obliquity, polyvocalism, self-reflexivity, and others of its own devising—present tense, conversational diction, unpolished voice quality, and a variety of emphases on the narrator's affinities with the audience and characters.

Yet the previous theoretical consensus on third-person voice-over narration is that unacceptable pretensions to authority are built into its structure. Bonitzer and Doane identify several interrelated qualities they see as inherent in the technique and automatically responsible for overweening power. Bonitzer states:

> Voice[-over] forbids questions about its bearer, its place, and its time. Commentary, in informing the image, [and] the image, in letting itself be invested by the commentary, censure such questions.
> This is not, one suspects, without ideological implications. The first of these implications is that the voice[-over] represents a power, that of disposing of the image and of what it reflects, from a space absolutely *other* with respect to that inscribed in the image track. *Absolutely other and absolutely indeterminate.* Because it rises from the field of the Other, the voice[-over] is assumed to know: this is the essence of its power.[17]

Doane similarly notes: "It is its radical otherness with respect to the diegesis which endows this voice with a certain authority. . . . It is precisely because the voice is not localizable, because it cannot be yoked to a body, that it is capable of interpreting the image, producing its truth." [18] Lack of body, anonymity, indeterminable time and place of narrating, immunity to criticism, and "radical otherness with respect to the diegesis": these are the inherent qualities credited with endowing the narrator with power and pretensions to truth. *The Naked City,* however, raises questions concerning both the constancy and inevitable ramifications of these qualities.

Certainly, it is the narrator's lack of a body that makes him so unearthly and that so readily prompts comparisons with the Lord. Yet we actually deal with disembodied voices—on the radio, on tape recordings, over public address systems, on the telephone—all the time in our daily lives without pausing in awe. Perhaps the distinction lies in the fact that generally the bodies of the people to whom we are listening are at least imaginarily recoverable; we can picture them in our mind's eye. But is seeing, or imagining, the narrator's body really such a crucial issue? After all, few viewers of *The Naked City* have ever seen a picture of Mark Hellinger, and thus most do not have any definite impression of what he looked like.

As for the narrator's name and the time and place of his discourse, this information is conventionally kept from the viewer, but what law decrees that these details must remain secret? We saw above that Mark Hellinger introduces himself in the first few moments of the film. One can also pick up certain minimal clues about his narrating time and space. But even if we knew whence the narrator was speaking, if we could see his surroundings and watch him in the act of narrating, would this automatically neutralize his power? Doane says that television newspeople can slip into voice-of-God narration because they are situated in the "non-space" of the studio,[19] but Mike

Wallace—who is anything but anonymous—sounds authoritative and all-knowing whether he is in the studio or out in the field, whether he is speaking on camera or off.

Bonitzer claims that if viewers cannot see a speaker on the screen and compare his words with his facial expressions and gestures, the narrator escapes "*la critique du regard*"; Bonitzer's argument implies that this speaker is thus immune to criticism.[20] But the *New Yorker* had no difficulty noticing and criticizing the shallowness of some of Mark Hellinger's pronouncements. If, by being off-screen, unseen, the voice-over narrator could truly coerce us, then why are we able to jeer at the narrator of *The March of Time?* * Why should critical acumen be restricted to visual scrutiny (why, again, should the visual track be favored over the aural?): what about "the critique of listening?" We never see the expositors of essays or the narrators of novels, and many of them cannot be yoked to identities or to bodies, yet they do not escape our searching evaluation of their intelligence and reliability.

Bonitzer and Doane seem to be lumping together the fact that most third-person narrators are frame narrators with the fact that they are heterodiegetic. The combination of these two factors is potent and certainly contributes to the voice-over's strangeness and ability to put on Olympian airs, but the first is less immutable and less important; after all, we do view television newspeople in the act of narrating, yet they do not lose their privilege to pontificate or to Know Everything and Be Everywhere; similarly, in Thornton Wilder's *Our Town,* the Stage Manager stands up in flesh and blood right before our eyes, yet he has divine knowledge and control over stage events.

The crux of the issue may be that, as Doane and Bonitzer state, the heterodiegetic narrator is *radically other with respect to the diegesis.* No one could gainsay this description: this otherness is inherent in the definition of such narration. When a narrator is not a character, not a participant in the story he or she relates, that narrator is not bound by the rules of plausibility that govern the characters: the narrator is superior to them, the shaper of their destinies. For some Marxist critics, this creates an ideological problem for documentaries in that when the story world, the diegesis, is supposed to equal The Real World, a narrator who is not homogeneous with his subjects, not bound by the rules that restrict them, can indeed seem untouched by history, extra-worldly.

Yet this privilege is not unique to documentary or fiction films, but rather equally inherent in every third-person narration, factual or fictional; oral, literary, or cinematic. In films without voice-over, the image-maker serves as the sole narrator, and he, too, is "radically other with respect to the diegesis" and in a position of knowledge and power. In narrated films this "otherness"

---

*We might keep in mind that our present ability to criticize *The March of Time* does not arise solely from our historical perspective. Pauline Kael reports in "Raising Kane" (*The Citizen Kane Book* [New York: Bantam, 1971], p. 81) that student audiences laughed at the newsreel's narrator in 1939, and presumably the whole country laughed at Welles's parody in 1941.

only seems exaggerated because voice-over is so obviously removed from the action and dialogue presented on the image track. But as we all recognize, the presence of rhetoric does not hinge upon the degree of overtness or covertness of the narrating "voice"; intrusive, loquacious narrators are no more manipulative and authoritarian than silent narrators—just more audible.

One could, of course, decree that films (or novels) use only homodiegetic narrators. According to the canons of plausibility, credible first-person narrators must be bound by human and historical limitations: such narrators should be only humanly wise, know only their own thoughts and feelings, and be constricted in time and space to their own experiences and surroundings. And indeed, some films use limited character-narrators or interviewees, but inevitably one finds that they are presented by a more powerful camera-narrator, and embedded within the more authoritative and more covert discourse of the film as a whole (*All About Eve* reveals this clearly). And when filmmakers or authors employ reliable first-person narrators and allow them to act as spokespersons for the entire text, it is curious how often such narrators slither into positions of unlimited knowledge and freedom indistinguishable from those of heterodiegetic narrators (think of narrating-Huw in *How Green Was My Valley*). Actually, I think, we need to revise our expectations regarding the power of first-person narrators; so many of them in both film and literature violate the canons of plausibility that these canons need to be extended and updated.

The *Oxford English Dictionary* tells us that *narrate* is "ultimately allied to Know." First-person or third, voice-over narrators are no more inherently knowledgeable, and consequently powerful, than any other kind of narrator—but also no less. However overt or covert, all narration requires knowledge, reveals biases, connotes power. There may in fact be something undemocratic about such power being concentrated in a single voice. Yet this monopoly appears unavoidable: I do not believe that the use of multiple narrators can ever convincingly provide the authentic polyvocalism that Bonitzer advocates. Watching the documentaries of the thirties and forties that use more than one voice on the narrating track, I again find myself unable to overlook the fact that these extra voices are only present through the will of the filmmakers and their spokesperson, the principal narrator.

Mary Louise Pratt helps us realize that the narrative act is grounded in a particular situation.[21] The narrator monopolizes the floor and takes away from audience members the "turn taking" rights that prevail in ordinary conversation; but the audience is not without compensatory powers. First of all, in most cases, attendance is voluntary (viewers usually go to films out of choice and, however little they exercise the option, they can always walk out). Secondly, the audience is endowed with the right to pass judgment (when the lights come up, all viewers immediately feel entitled to pronounce their critical review).

Storytelling is a human activity (how many films or novels has the Lord actually narrated recently?). I see it not as a pernicious threat but as a privilege and responsibility. The moral and political questions concerning voice-over do not revolve around its unique essence, but around how filmmakers use it—what they have the narrator say, and in what manner. "Voice of God" narration is due as much to pretentious scripting and the casting of sonorous, stentorian voices as to factors inherent in the form itself. And scripts and styles are changeable; the production history of *The Naked City* demonstrates that each use of narration depends on a multiplicity of factors: the state of the country, the film industry, and film technology; and the backgrounds, sensibilities, and politics of the people involved.

Strange that the very recognition of illusionism anathematized by the Jamesians at the turn of the century is now what strikes us as the more honest pose; we want the filmic discourse to acknowledge itself and its perspective, to let us hear and judge its voice, to open itself up for our scrutiny. One can allow for this kind of scrutiny through any number of manipulations of script or execution; we may discover through further research on previous films or through current experimentation that some strategies are more successful than others. We must remember, however, that these strategies are themselves "rhetorical": we might question whether any of those used in *The Naked City* really neutralize the narrator's privileged standpoint, or whether all they do is make it more palatable and forestall criticism of open didacticism.

Gender

In terms of ideology, we now notice that, as Susan Lanser puts it, "The question of silence sometimes becomes as crucial as the question of voice; 'who does not speak' is as revealing as 'who speaks?' " [22] Although I do not agree with Bonitzer and Doane that casting women as third-person narrators would essentially compromise such a narrator's power or knowledge, they are right to raise the issue of gender. It is initially startling to realize that within the boundaries of this study, women have almost never been used as heterodiegetic narrators. I have found but one example of an American fiction film with such a narrator; my sampling is incomplete, but even if one were to locate more obscure examples, these would only be exceptions that prove the rule.

It is not that women do not narrate in the cinema, because they serve as character-narrators quite frequently, perhaps nearly as frequently as men. Moreover, woman can be found as third-person narrators in other forums. They have served as the narrators of documentaries, both during World War II and in contemporary works. On television, women do sometimes serve as third-person narrators of commercials, and they can be found both as news correspondents, and, during the fifties, as hostesses of dramatic anthology series.

What accounts for the plenitude of certain types of female narrators and the paucity of others? One major factor is the nature of the material—female narrators are likely to be confined to a certain domestic or personal ghetto. As first-person narrators they narrate their own life stories or their own memories in "women's films," adaptations, and occasional *noirs;* their area of knowledge is generally constricted to what they have personally experienced and to what is presumed to be of interest to primarily female viewers. By the same token, commercials narrated by women are generally for women's products, such as perfume or hair coloring, not for cars or financial planning, and women in television news have had to struggle for hard-news assignments.

Another reason for this exclusion is that, as previous discussion has indicated, a heterodiegetic narrator has a particular position vis-à-vis the text as a whole. As Linda Dégh notes in the course of her work on folktales, "In general, the women remain within the family circle; they tell their stories to children or grandchildren or other adults in the family; the men, on the other hand, seek the big audiences, the publicity." She concludes, "Doubtless it is the men who are the storytellers among European peoples."[23] If the "voice of the storyteller" in Western society has traditionally been male, it is hardly surprising that the "voice of the image-maker" should traditionally be male also. To the extent that the flesh-and-blood image-makers of feature films have nearly exclusively been male, it has been unthinkable for their mouthpieces to speak in higher registers. And *The March of Time* stereotype has only exacerbated the situation: because third-person narrators have been allowed and encouraged to make sweeping pronouncements about human nature and society (especially, one realizes, in such "male" genres as war films and semi-documentaries), the role has been automatically assigned to authoritative male voices.

Finally, in recent years feminist and psychoanalytic critics have argued that classical cinema is predicated on the male spectator's gaze at on-screen women, a gaze they relate to both voyeurism and fetishism. This "gaze" serves both to objectify and eroticize women, and finally to dominate them.[24] Similarly, Molly Haskell argues, "the conception of woman as idol, art object, icon, and visual entity is, after all, the first principle of the aesthetic of film as a visual medium."[25]

With these arguments in mind, perhaps the difference between television hostesses and newswomen on the one hand, and cinematic third-person voice-over on the other, is that while we initially or eventually see Loretta Young or Jane Pauley on camera, in film the narrators are almost always *extra*diegetic, and thus never appear on screen. Haskell argues that the film industry has "preferred its women malleable and pleasing to the eye; and . . . like men the world over, felt deep down that women should be seen but not heard."[26] If a woman were *heard* but never *seen*, she would escape the limiting, possessive, and erotic scrutiny to which she may be subjected when her image has been captured by the camera and offered to the gaze of the spectators.

There are films that delay yoking a female voice-over to a body; Henry Hathaway's *Kiss of Death* (1947), which initially leads us to believe that the voice is heterodiegetic, only to reveal belatedly that it belongs to the protagonist's wife, is a prime example. But I have found only two *never*-seen female narrators in American fiction film. In Mankiewicz's *A Letter to Three Wives* (1949), the narrator, Addie Ross, exists on the same level of reality as the other characters, she is homodiegetic, yet she figures in the film only as narrating-I: no experiencing-I ever appears on the screen. Interestingly, Addie is the villain of the piece. She is portrayed as a sadistic home-wrecker, and all of the other characters' remarks about her emphasize her sexuality. The film's final image of a champagne glass breaking symbolizes the shattering of her presumptuous powers.

The second is found in a recent release, the 1986 adaptation of Jean Auel's *The Clan of the Cave Bear,* directed by Michael Chapman. Here, finally, is a case of female third-person voice-over, spoken by the actress Salome Jens. Perhaps this film is the exception because the novel's author and the story's protagonist are both female, and its screenwriter, John Sayles, is known for his liberal and non-sexist sensibilities, and its themes are pointedly feminist.

The barriers against women serving as third-person narrators in feature films have been so many and so high that their thorough exclusion ultimately seems overdetermined. If a woman were to serve as a third-person narrator, not only would she be allowed dominion over the public sphere as opposed to private, not only would she potentially wield great power and authority, not only would she speak as the film's image-maker, but she would escape being objectified or eroticized. Yet *The Clan of the Cave Bear,* in which the narration seems so matter-of-fact and so unradical, leads me to believe that the barriers are crumbling, and will continue to do so, and that the days when one gender dominated this narratorial posture are over.

5

Irony in Voice-Over Films

In *The Nature of Narrative,* Scholes and Kellogg note that the Jamesians' real complaint against the literary intrusive narrator stems from the fact that he is supposed to be totally reliable. Thus, they state, "a narrator who is not in some way suspect, who is not in some way open to ironic scrutiny, is what the modern temper finds least bearable." [1] This study has been leading up to irony in order to demonstrate how filmmakers open up their narrators to this scrutiny.

To understand the relationship of voice-over to irony, however, we must examine the technique in even more detail. In literature the interplay between the narrator's comments and the story events from one sentence or phrase to the next is indubitably rich and complicated, but the narrator's remarks must perforce come before or after the instance to which he or she refers, and both story and discourse are transmitted through a single sign system—language. Voice-over narration, however, occurs *simultaneously* with a moving image or sequence of images conveying all kinds of information to the viewer via dramatic activity, camera position and movement, lighting, scenery, properties, dialogue, and music. Accordingly, the relationships between the verbal narration and the images/action portrayed on the screen are extraordinarily complex and require a close look.

The Interplay between Narration and Scenic Presentation

As Claudia Gorbman points out,[2] critics such as Kracauer discuss the soundtrack in terms of binary categories: a given instance is pigeonholed as syn-

Figure 3

Degree of Correspondence between Narration and Images

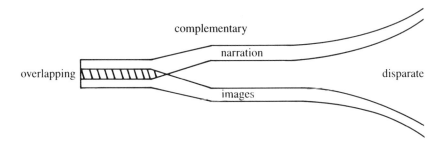

chronous or asynchronous in relation to the images, its information "parallel" or in "counterpoint" to that presented visually. By definition, voice-over is always asynchronous, but one runs into difficulty with the other two vague categories. Determining whether the information conveyed by the two tracks is "parallel" or "in counterpoint" is a problematic undertaking: what, after all, does one judge—the data conveyed in each, or the manner in which that data is conveyed? How does one compare connotations and denotations of totally different sign systems?

Well, very subjectively. One can only look for cooperation, harmonies, or dissonances on several levels. To begin with, narration/image relationships may be more accurately described if we abandon the model of binary opposition, and imagine a *continuous* graph recording the degree to which the two tracks correspond. At one end, we find "overlapping" narration; at the other, a high degree of disparity, even contradiction, between the two tracks. The majority of narrated sequences fall into a large middle ground, where the two tracks work in tandem, yet augment each other's meaning. I shall call the interplay between narration and scenic presentation in such cases "complementary," but one should keep in mind that a given "complementary" pairing can lie close to either extreme (Figure 3).

Overlapping pairings were discussed in chapter 1 during our look at "redundancy," where I noted that strictly speaking, different information must always be provided by the different tracks. The closest they ever come may be those instances where a voice speaks aloud the same words simultaneously printed on the screen. (Although even here a definite and potentially major discrepancy exists between the sound of voice and the look of the print.) Such oral/print narration is not uncommon. At its best, it highlights time-honored words, or conveys that this narrative has a written epic situation; at its worst, it seems to betray the filmmaker's doubt that the audience knows how to listen or read without help.

Moving a little further right on the graph in Figure 3, when the screen offers scenery and action instead of printed titles, the viewer is faced with judging more disparate sign systems, but he or she can still easily recognize when the narration describes actions or objects simultaneously visible on the screen. Such overlapping is a tool for emphasis. The catch, as was noted in chapter 1, is that the subject must seem worthy of this particular emphasis: commercials that overlap narration and action to burn their messages into the viewer's mind can be especially irritating. But the overlap during the opening of *The Magnificent Ambersons* is surely both deliberate and justified. Orson Welles's off-screen voice describes a way of life that is simultaneously illustrated on the screen: we both see and hear about the streetcar waiting for its passengers and the fashions of the late nineteenth century are both modeled and verbally described. This slow pace mimics the relaxed life-style, emphasizes the importance of this exposition, and heightens our awareness of the image-maker's presence and control.

"Overlapping" narration shades imperceptibly into "complementary" pairings. Depending on one's words-versus-image bias, one could say that in these cases, the visuals illustrate the narration, or that the narration identifies the images; actually, recalling Barthes's discussion in "The Rhetoric of the Image,"[3] each track *anchors* the meaning of the other, pinning down possible ambiguities. Furthermore, each track *extends* the meaning of the other by providing information not accessible, or not highlighted, in its companion.

Take, for example, the totally unexceptional opening of Billy Wilder's *The Apartment* (1960). We see a moving aerial shot of skyscrapers, a cityscape next to a river. A spectator might recognize the architecture and spot the United Nations or the Empire State Building in the background, but the buildings go by quickly. It is the off-screen narration that defines time and place:

On November 1st, 1959 the population
of New York City was 8,042,783.

The narration informs us this is "New York," the image informs us what "New York" looks like—big, gray, stony buildings. This aerial shot, a sweeping survey of a big metropolis, continues, and the narration continues with sweeping statistics also stressing the city's size: "If you laid all those people end to end, figuring an average height of 5′6½″, they would reach from Times Square to Karachi, Pakistan. I know facts like this because I work for an insurance company—" Here, there is a dissolve: the new street-level shot captures a modern glassy building at right angles to an old-fashioned stone building with lion statues guarding the stairs. The stone building and the lions look interesting, but the narration directs our attention to the glass structure:

—Consolidated Life of New York; we're one of the top five companies in the country. Our home office has 31,259 employees, which is more than the entire population of . . . uh . . . Natchez, Mississippi.

As the narration tells us how important and large the company is, the camera pans up the glass skyscraper—its impenetrability, massiveness, and soullessness further define Consolidated Life (no life here); the shot also keeps our thoughts from straying to Natchez. Another dissolve. We see a large interior, an office with scores of people working at desks aligned in rows, stretching as far as we can see. The people look busy and joyless. Narration:

I work on the nineteenth floor, Ordinary Policy Department, Premium Accounting Division, desk number 861.

These words explain the visuals, telling us where we are; the images illustrate the narration, by showing what the nineteenth floor is like. A cut (not a dissolve, the pace is quickening), to a close up of Jack Lemmon at a desk punching an adding machine. The camera is slightly to the side of him; the shot catches his face in profile.

My name is C. C. Baxter, C. for Calvin, C. for Clifford—however, most people call me 'Bud.'

The close-up anchors the voice, the "I," and the name to a face, a man, an actor; simultaneously, the narration anchors the face/man/actor to a name, a job, and a dramatic role.

At one moment during this short sequence, the information provided visually and verbally overlaps: the shot shows us we're in New York by focusing on the distinctive skyline, and Baxter explicitly names the location. At other moments they are very close, but not actually overlapping: while we could recognize the Empire State Building as an iconic sign for New York, we could not possibly know that the glass skyscraper houses the fictitious Consolidated Life without help. Sometimes, as when Baxter mentions Karachi or Natchez, the two tracks are miles apart. Clearly, however, the two tracks are working together, complementing each other, the words naming the images, the images connecting the words with concrete physical objects. Together they orient the viewer in time and space, acquaint us with Baxter's personality (his ordinariness, his command of little facts and figures, his small ambitions and vanities), and stress the size and coldness of his city and his company.

This opening section exemplifies the fact that all complementary pairings of narration and images provide more information than would have been available from either alone. New knowledge is created by the juxtaposition of the two (Eisenstein would call it "vertical montage"). To take another example, in *Mildred Pierce* Mildred's narrating voice remarks, "At first it bothered Monte [her lover] to take money from me, then it became a habit with him." The shot accompanying this statement does not show Monte taking a check from her, instead, we see a sheaf of bills from fancy men's clothing stores. The unspoken implication is that these are Monte's bills, that this is what he's spending her hard-earned money on. The combination of picture and narration forcefully reveals Monte's profligacy without stating it explicitly on either track: it quietly leads the viewer to make the connection himself or herself.

In many respects the narration and the images of *The Apartment* are in harmony. For one thing, they maintain a certain harmony of scale; they move together from the large to the small, from the city of New York to the problems of one little guy at desk 861. This tendency towards harmony of scale is quite pronounced in fiction films; descriptions of cities are commonly matched with long-shots, descriptions of people or of states of mind with close-ups.

Moreover, in this example, the narration and the images are carefully timed together. Two of the cuts occur at the end of sentences, one at the end of a phrase. Editors with whom I have spoken claim that there are no set rules for determining the timing of the narration vis-à-vis the images; sometimes one cuts so "you see it before you say it," sometimes so that "you say it before you see it," sometimes so that "you say it as you see it." The more closely the two tracks correspond, the less suspense or tension created. This opening leaves us hanging only on one issue: we hear the voice refer to himself, but the "I" is not identified, not anchored, for three shots, until we see Baxter and he

Rebecca. Mrs. De Winter [voice-over]: Last night I dreamed I went to Manderly again. . . .

. . . And finally, there was Manderly, Manderly, secretive and silent.

The Lady from Shanghai. Michael O'Hara [voice-over]: When I start to make a fool of myself, there's very little can stop me. . . .

introduces himself to us. This delay creates a minor amount of suspense, which is resoundingly terminated with the fourth shot.

Finally, one does not notice any obvious discrepancy in the tonality or coloration of *The Apartment*'s two tracks. One of the hallmarks of complementary narration is a general harmony between the words, the tone of voice, the attitude of the narrator, the style of the images, and the mood of the music. Thus, in an extreme and obvious case, *Rebecca* begins with Joan Fontaine narrating her dream about returning to Manderly while Hitchcock mimics her dreamy tone with a gliding camera (simulating her physical point of view), exaggerated scenery and melodramatic lighting.

Describing typical interactions between narration and images helps us pinpoint ways in which filmmakers break with established patterns. Orson Welles violates harmony of scale in *The Lady from Shanghai:* the film begins with a long-shot of the New York skyline, but instead of the narration providing a "This is New York" exposition, it jumps right into Michael O'Hara's consciousness. Furthermore, when editors decide to cut the narration and image out of step with each other, disparities can be created, forcing the viewer to scramble to match up the verbal and visual information. (The avant-garde filmmaker Hollis Frampton takes temporal mismatching to extremes in *(nostalgia),* in which the narration perpetually refers not to the image currently on the screen but to the one that will be shown a few minutes later.) Finally, film-makers can easily move away from harmony of tone: in *The Naked City*, Hellinger's wry comments often create a slight frisson in the context of the pseudodocumentary style.

Such disparities may not create definite contrasts, but they can engender a greater or lesser feeling of disquiet. More major disparities are created by having the two tracks' tonalities clash openly, or even by having the signifieds of one track contradict those of the other. These cases will be covered after a general consideration of irony in narrated films.

Voice-Over's Contribution to Cinematic Irony

Voice-over narration extends film's ironic capabilities.

Irony has now become such a large concept that theorists must constantly break it down into subcategories, yet in his attempt to give a general definition, D. C. Muecke highlights the fact that it involves a double-layered structure—on the lower level we find the situation as it appears to the victim of the irony or as it is deceptively presented by the ironist, and on the upper level, the situation as it appears to the observer who has been clued in, or to the ironist himself.[4] Now non-voice-over films have always been able to present certain types of ironies within their stories: "verbal irony" by the characters (Walter Burns's and Hildy Johnson's repartee in *His Girl Friday*), "dramatic irony" (in *The 39 Steps* Richard Hannay strives desperately to reach Professor Jordan for help, only to discover that Jordan is the chief villain), or "tragic irony" (Ratzo Rizzo dies just as he arrives in Florida in *Midnight Cowboy*). But because films without voice-over are told solely by a silent image-maker, they are limited in the kinds of irony that can surround *the telling of the film*.

A comparison may help explain this limitation. Scholes and Kellogg note that the traditional oral narrative, which consisted rhetorically of "a teller, his story, and an implied audience," was also limited in terms of irony. The narrators were invariably authoritative and reliable; only minimal irony could be created by the narrator and the audience "together know[ing] the characters of the story as they could not possibly know each other or even themselves." In other words, an oral narrator could be an ironist, but he could not be the victim of irony. However, written narratives added to the equation an author (who stands outside the text), and transmute the flesh-and-blood storyteller into an *imitation* or *representation* of a storyteller. Because the source of the narrative is now doubled, and because the act of storytelling is now a part of the text (this holds true even when the literary narrator is heterodiegetic, but is especially obvious when he or she is a character in the story), an ironic distance can be opened up between narrator and the implied author.[5]

In non-voice-over films, the image-maker can be ironic to a certain extent. He can wink at the audience over the characters' heads by catching the word "Rosebud" just before the sled burns in *Citizen Kane,* or by intercutting shots of a prancing peacock with shots of Kerensky in *October;* he can use lighting, camera framing, and editing to comment on the characters—he can certainly add ironic musical scoring. But as expressive as these instruments may be, the image-maker is hampered—even in comparison with the traditional oral story-teller—by his silence. Moreover, like an oral storyteller, he is condemned to constant reliability, constant authority; I can think of no methods by which an image-maker could cast grave or persistent doubts upon his own adequacy or truthfulness. Even if the film contained discrepancies between the image and sound tracks, lapses of continuity, or other distortions or interruptions, I believe that the viewer interprets these anomalies as purposeful, as a deliberate flouting of convention (witness Godard's films), rather than as the unconscious, inadvertent revelations of an inadequate narrator.[6]

Adding voice-over narration, however, alters the situation. Now the teller has a voice and can employ all kinds of verbal ironies. Moreover, now we find a doubling of the source of the narrative, an image-maker and an imitation storyteller; thus, should the filmmaker wish, he or she can create an ironic distance between these two sources. Finally, for either purpose, the adding of the narration track over the image track creates a pliable, double-layered structure, perfect for creating ironic disparities or contradictions.

As implied above, filmmakers can exploit the ironic potential of voice-over narration in two ways. One is to keep the connection between the image-maker and the narrator tight, to maintain the illusion that the narrator is the presenter of the entire film (or at least of his story-within-a-story), but give this narrator an ironic temperament. In this event, the narrator will be seen as creating and controlling any disparities between narration and images/action. The other choice is to widen the gap, throw the narrator's telling into question, make him or her out to be more or less unreliable. Here the image-maker would use clashes between narration and scenic presentation to compromise the narrator and to break the viewer's provisional belief in that narrator's responsibility for the text.

One might expect that superior, ironic narrators would be heterodiegetic, godlike, and all-knowing, yet this does not always hold true. A first-person frame narrator such as Joe Gillis in *Sunset Boulevard* can be extremely ironical; so, too, can an embedded narrator such as Henry Van Cleves in Lubitsch's *Heaven Can Wait* (1943). By the same token, one might predict that compromised, unreliable narrators would always be characters within the diegesis, but such positioning is not axiomatic. Many films parody documentary narration: *The More and Merrier* and *Casablanca* offer prime examples of heterodiegetic narrators whom the image-maker and the viewer evaluate and find wanting: they are the victims of the image-maker's irony.[7]

Ironic Narrators

Ironic narrators' temperaments sometimes emerge solely or primarily through their manner of speaking (which is hardly surprising, since character revelation is one of the basic functions of voice-over narration). Philip Marlowe's cynical comments in *Murder, My Sweet*—"It had a nice front yard," he says of the enormous Grayle mansion. "Cozy. OK for the average family. You need a compass to go to the mailbox"—are ironic in and of themselves.

Often, however, a narrator's irony, or the impact of his irony, comes from the interplay between the commentary and the images on the screen. One classic example is John Huston's documentary *The Battle of San Pietro* (1943), which describes one of the costliest battles of World War II. Much of the irony comes from Huston's canny pairings of shots and verbal narration. Over images of horrendous destruction, the narrator offers guidebook phrases: "A farming community" (shot of blasted fields). "Patron, St. Peter" (shot of ruined statue). "Point of interest: St. Peter's, 1438" (shot of bombed church). "Note—interesting treatment of chancel" (panning shot showing the bomb craters in the chancel).[8] Ironic understatement in the face of horrors crops up in many other documentaries, and also in fiction films as divergent as *Kiss of Death* and *Apocalypse Now*. The counterpoint between the casualness of the narration and the brutality displayed on the screen can be chilling.

On the other hand, ironic narrators can engender humorous disparitites by overinflating their commentary. In *Cannery Row*, the narrator (John Huston again) describes the Great Frog Hunt in terms appropriate to some momentous occasion:

> During the millennia that men have hunted frogs, a pattern of hunt and parry has developed. . . . The rules of the game require the frog to bide his time, to the final flicker of a second, and then to jump into the water, swim to the bottom, and wait for things to blow over. This is the way it's done, the way it's always been done. Frogs don't resent this. But how could they have foreseen the horror that followed?

A good deal of the sequence's charm lies in the writing, in the anthropomorphizing of the frogs ("Frogs don't resent this"), but the irony is further compounded by these words being spoken over extreme close-ups of frogs hanging around on their lily pads in the dappled moonlight. The frogs look so ridiculous—so incapable of participating as equal antagonists in a complex battle strategy—and the lighting makes the scene so peaceful, so idyllic (setting the frogs and the viewer up for the tennis-racket-horror to follow), that the narrator's grandiose description comes across as delightfully incongruous. "Overinflation" crops up frequently in comedies and in films dealing with everyday life; one can find other examples, for instance, in Billy Wilder's

The Seven Year Itch (1955), and Henry Koster's *Mr. Hobbs Takes a Vacation* (1962).

Overinflation and understatement work through obvious tonal discrepancies between the commentary and the scenic presentation; paradoxically, narrators also create irony by having their comments correspond too closely with screen action. The anonymous narrator of Truffaut's *Jules et Jim* plays with a combination of redundancy and understatement. He describes Jules and Jim's actions in minute detail while we see these actions on the screen, and resolutely refuses to take the slightest note of the absurdity of the two friends' deeds. Like the stereotype of the unflappable butler, he recounts their dashing off to an Adriatic island to worship the statue resembling Catherine—in identical suits no less—completely matter-of-factly.

Other films illustrate "romantic irony"—that is, the deliberate calling into question or demolishing of a work's dramatic illusion. Godard's films could hardly be more self-conscious: ten minutes into *Bande à part* (1964) he offers "a few clues for late-comers" in the audience. But this kind of cinematic irony was hardly invented by the New Wave: the narrators of *The Solid Gold Cadillac* and *Tom Jones* also frequently call attention to their positions as story-tellers (the latter remarking, over a scene of Tom sporting amorously with Molly, "It shall be our custom to leave such scenes where taste, decorum, and the censor dictate"). Verbal recognitions of the narrator-puppeteer's control of the film may be employed in tandem with special manipulations of the image track, such as tuning out the sound, freezing the frame, irising in or out, elaborate editing, or darkening the screen.

Unreliable Narrators

We now reach the other possibility: a narrator being limited or unreliable, and thus becoming the victim of the image-maker's irony. As Wayne Booth has taught us, we judge a narrator's reliability on whether he speaks and acts in accordance with the norms of the work as a whole;[9] thus we must consider many factors besides the relationships of words and images. In Scorsese's *Taxi Driver,* whatever the interplay between Travis Bickle's narrating comments and the shots may be, his psychotic behaviour is sufficient to break our faith in him as a trustworthy guide, and to hold him up for our condemnation and pity. The context of the story as a whole also explains the frequent unreliability of narrators who are not insane, just in love. In Charles Vidor's *Gilda* (1946), for instance, we smile to ourselves when Johnny Farrell comes up with all sorts of justifications for marching into Gilda's bedroom except the real one. Our insight stems not from disparate pairings of the voice-over and the images, but from preceding events and love story conventions.

Nonetheless, filmmakers often exploit disparities between narration and

The Marrying Kind. Chester [voice-over]: Sure enough, there they were, giving us the eye, and we come right between them. But we kept right on walking, we never looked around.

scenic presentation to compromise their narrators. Sometimes the narrator is mistaken, or overly subjective, and the images reveal his limitations. In George Cukor's comedy *The Marrying Kind* (1952), the possibility of biased storytelling and/or biased perception becomes a major theme. The film takes place in a divorce court where Florence (Judy Holliday) and Chester Keefer (Aldo Ray) are explaining to the judge why they want to dissolve their marriage. At the beginning, the wise woman judge notes, "There are three sides to every story, yours, his, and the truth." Florence and Chester proceed to narrate their stories over flashbacks, and we hear their biased interpretations, yet the camera shows only the truth. Thus, for instance, Chet grumbles that the family was never happy—but we see a shot of them laughing uproariously around the kitchen table—or claims that in his initial meeting with Florence, he and his buddy never turned to look back at the girls, but we see them doing exactly that.

Similarly, in *Cat Ballou* the narrator is split into two people who continually contradict each other (e.g., Cole claims that Cat has "the eyes of an angel," and then Kaye growls, "Bites like the devil"), leaving the viewer doubting them both. Even when the two men sing ensemble, they still present the stuff of ballads about the Old West, not historical fact. They sing:

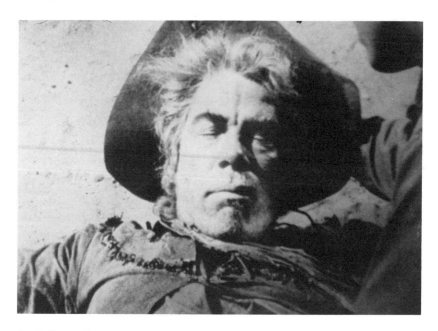

Cat Ballou. "The eyes of a killer"?

> Then there came to town
> A gun deadly and frightening,
> A gun quicker than lightning,
> Fastest gun you've seen;
> It was the gun in the hand of
> Steel-eyed Kid Shalleen.

Moments later the camera shows The Truth: Kid Shalleen (Lee Marvin), a degenerate drunk, falling off the stagecoach into the street.

Indeed, when words and images absolutely contradict each other, the images seem always to be the truth-tellers, and filmmakers will go to certain lengths to protect their image track's reliability. In reference to forties films such as *Laura* and *Mildred Pierce,* Guido Fink notes that a "silently accepted convention seems to state that images and visualized actions, though subservient to the word, may omit something but never distort the truth. . . . A curious balance or compensation rules that oral narration—conscious, subjective, deliberate—helps us to understand and rationalize events, but may be lying; narrated stories—that is, represented, shown events—may be partial, disturbing, incomplete, but never false." [10]

As evidence that this convention applies today, look at a recent Agatha Christie thriller, *Evil under the Sun* (Hamilton, 1982), where each of the suspects recounts his alibi to Hercule Poirot via a voice-over flashback. The two murderers, naturally, lie. However, at the denouement, when Poirot recounts what really happened, the thrifty filmmakers are able to take the same shots shown in the murderers' flashbacks and reedit them—the shots that the audience saw originally were *not* false, they were just partial and anchored by verbal lies.

But the image's reliability is not essential; it is just a convention, and conventions are made to be broken. Alfred Hitchcock did just this in *Stage Fright* (1950), which includes the famous "lying flashback," a flashback in which the scenic presentation colludes with the narrator's false account of events. This flashback, which is placed quite early in the film, convinces both the heroine and the audience of one character's innocence, and a great many viewers—especially critics—were outraged to find out that he was actually the killer and that he and Hitchcock had lied to them.[11] Hitchcock never repeated this experiment, and it has not caught on in American cinema; for whatever reasons, the underlying need to believe in the reality of the scenic presentation in general and the photographic image in particular is too pervasive, too strong here. Foreign filmmakers seem to be more willing to place the truth status of the image in doubt: recall Kurosawa's *Rashomon,* Resnais's *L'Année dernière à Marienbad,* and Robbe-Grillet's *L'Homme qui ment.*

Is it possible to reverse the convention completely and have the camera lie to the viewer while the narrator tells the truth verbally? To put it another way, can we ever believe that an image-maker is less reliable than his creation, the narrator? To my knowledge, *An American in Paris* (Minnelli, 1951) comes closest to such a reversal. Its opening section is narrated by three characters, each of whom introduces himself to the audience. Each time, instead of the camera focusing on the right person, it first frames some innocent stranger, forcing the narrating character to correct it. For example, when the camera should be presenting Jerry Mulligan (Gene Kelly), and instead captures a young man and woman on the floor below him in the midst of an embrace, Mulligan redirects it: "No, not there, one flight up"; the camera then obligingly cranes upwards and frames Kelly, who now approvingly notes, "Voilà!" But even here the camera's "mistake" does not indicate unreliability. The blunders turn out to have been motivated by a higher purpose; the innocent strangers demonstrate what each of the principal characters lacks—e.g., Jerry needs a girl friend. As Mary Louise Pratt explains, because works of art have gone through rigorous selection and preparation, the audience feels confident that discrepancies and ironies arise from the creator's deliberate "flouting" of conventions.[12] Accordingly, whenever a discrepancy arises between the scenic presentation and the narration we seek for—and if necessary, invent—a rationale behind the discrepancy, assuming that the image-maker is still firmly at the wheel.

At any rate, not all unreliable narrators are liars or murderers. We take some narrators with a pinch of salt just because they are naive or limited. In these cases, the verbal narration and the scenic presentation do not necessarily contradict each other outright, but one notes certain continual discrepancies in tone, and these discrepancies loom larger and seem more and more significant as the film proceeds.

Two films by Terence Malick present the classic models of this type of narration. *Badlands* (1974) follows sixteen-year-old Holly (Sissy Spacek) and her boyfriend, Kit (Martin Sheen), an unbalanced young man on a cross-country killing spree. Holly narrates this violent story in a monotone, relying on clichés. "It's not the mark of a diminished, pulp-fed mind . . . but of the 'innocent abroad,'" Malick has explained. "When people express what is most important to them, it often comes out in clichés. That doesn't make them laughable; it's something tender about them. As though in struggling to reach what's most personal about them they could only come up with what's most public." [13] Holly's perceptions and her idiom cannot provide adequate explanations of Kit's actions or her own feelings. For example, over a montage of Kit feeding hogs, we hear:

> Kit went to work in the feedlot, while I carried on with my studies. Little by little we fell in love. As I'd never been popular in school and didn't have a lot of personality, I was surprised that he took such a liking to me, especially when he could have had any other girl in town if he'd given it half a try.

Holly isn't lying—she's just completely limited by her clichés, and innocently blind to Kit's craziness. The visuals don't contradict her statements, they just highlight their inappropriateness by silently muttering "Hogwash!" In *Days of Heaven* (1978) Malick again employs a young girl as narrator; this story, set on a Texas farm in 1916, involves a tragic love triangle. The narrator (Linda Manz) is the little sister of one of the participants. Unlike Holly, Little Sister sees what's going on around her with extreme clarity—she is preternaturally wise. Nevertheless her narration makes us pause; she says such things as: "There was people sufferin' of pain and hunger. Such people. Their tongues were hangin' out of their mouths," and "Nobody's perfect. There was never a perfect person around. You just have half-angel and half-devil in you." Irony is engendered by an ignorant child's having such knowledge to begin with, by her cracked voice and expressionless, laconic delivery—which makes no distinction between her childish whims and her mature moral judgments, and by the contrast between her (accurate) verbalization of human pain and suffering and the piercing beauty of both the Almendros-Wexler cinematography and Morricone's musical score. In Malick's films the narration prompts uneasy laughter; we know that we cannot accept the narrator's statements at face value, and yet we do not know where to set our feet. And throughout both films, the audience becomes acutely aware that someone else, someone wiser—the image-maker—is actually presenting both the story and the purported storyteller.

The Question of Reliability
in *Barry Lyndon*

Let us turn to Stanley Kubrick's *Barry Lyndon* (1975) as a case study of irony and degrees of reliability in a narrated film. In this instance we do not have to weigh the contributions of various creative participants or untangle a complicated production history; Kubrick wrote the screenplay himself and personally supervised every detail of its three-year, $11 million production, basically telling Warner Brothers that they could take it or leave it.[14] We have only one major influence to consider: Kubrick's source, William Makepeace Thackeray's *The Luck of Barry Lyndon,* first published as a serial in 1844. Although differences exist between the plots of the novel and the film, both follow the exploits of the title character, an Irishman of a genteel, but impoverished, family, over several decades of the mid eighteenth century. They trace his impulsive and dishonest early adventures in love and war, his rise to wealth and position through his marriage to the widowed Lady Lyndon, and his decline into poverty and loneliness owing to his squandering of his wife's fortune, the disdain of his noble acquaintances, the enmity of his stepson, and the death of his son.[15]

What is particularly unusual and interesting about this film's voice-over is that Kubrick does not use it to recreate the narrative structure of the novel. Thackeray wrote his *Barry Lyndon* in the first person: Barry narrates from the vantage point of his destitute old age in Fleet Street Prison. The novel's narrator is a highly unreliable rogue who changes little, if at all, through the course of the story; he is so consistently full of conceit and stupidity that it is easy to see through his statements to detect the implied author's irony. In the 1844 text Thackeray made Barry's failings even more blatant by having the purported editor of Barry's memoirs, one George Savage Fitzboodle, add footnotes pointing out the correct interpretation of the protagonist's words and behavior. (These footnotes were, however, dropped from the 1856 edition.) Now as *Lolita* (1961) and *A Clockwork Orange* (1971) indicate, Kubrick was no stranger to unreliable first-person voice-over. But Barry does not narrate the film—instead an anonymous, heterodiegetic voice (Michael Hordern) assumes this duty. Rather than having the voice-over serve as a window into the principal character and as inadvertent self-revelation, Kubrick uses it for ironic commentary upon the hero and eighteenth-century aristocratic society.

And this commentary plays a crucial role in our experience of the film. Kubrick's vision of the eighteenth century is of a society straightjacketed by artificial civility. Civility cloaks the worst of misdeeds: Barry removes his stepson from the presence of company to beat him viciously by saying to his wife, "Dearest, will you excuse Lord Bullingdon and me for a few minutes; we have something to discuss in private"; the highwayman who robs Barry of everything he possesses introduces himself with courtly grace; gamblers accept enormous losses with airy shows of indifference; duelists fight with ritualized barbarity. The narrator's function in the film is to pierce through the polite posturings and romantic self-delusions of the characters, to lift off their society's veneer.

Often this narrator accomplishes his task through his words alone; he juxtaposes verbal incongruities masterfully. He speaks of Barry's resolutions being "steadfastly held for a whole week"; calls King Frederick of Prussia "great and illustrious" in the same breath as he reveals that this monarch highjacks civilians and impresses them into his army; and summarizes Barry's courtship of Lady Lyndon by noting, "To make a long story short, six hours after they met, the lady was in love."

The narrator also conveys his message through careful conjunction of his comments with particulars of the image track. He overinflates his description of Barry's crush on Nora, running on in purplish prose:

> First love, what a change it makes in a lad. What a magnificent secret it is that
> he carries about with him. The tender passion gushes instinctively out of a man's
> heart; he loves as a bird sings, or a wind blows, from nature.

The scene offers Barry and Nora playing cards; after the first sentence the camera cuts to a mid-shot and then a close-up of her. In these shots Nora (Gay Hamilton) is presented very unflatteringly: her expression is stern, her ears stick out, her hairline is uneven, her cheeks slightly pockmarked. The conjunction of words and images is funny and creates a contrast between Barry's naive and overblown affection and the worthlessness of its object; viewers are not taken by surprise when his cousin turns out to be faithless.

In the example above, the narrator's commentary presents a romantic cliché, which the images debunk. More typically, however, the images offer a beautiful exterior, apparently calling for a sentimental reaction from the viewer, which the narrator's statements totally undercut. The most shocking instance occurs when Barry parts from Lischen, a German woman with whom he has had a brief love affair. The blond, innocent-looking woman appears heartbroken as they embrace and Barry mounts his horse. The scene is touching: two attractive lovers, sunshine through green leaves, romantic music, a final good-by in the midst of war's insecurities. But the narrator remarks:

> A lady who set her heart on a lad in uniform, must prepare to change lovers
> very quickly or her life will be but a sad one. This heart of Lischen's was like
> many a neighboring town, and had been stormed and occupied several times
> before Barry came to invest it.

The images would have the viewer believe in the singularity and purity of their liaison; the narrator provides a more cynical perspective.

At times the narrator speaks very sympathetically of the characters, but the narration generally serves to distance us from them and from the action, and the narrator habitually destroys suspense by forewarning us of events well before they occur. Moreover, during two highly emotional scenes—Lord Lyndon's heart attack and Lady Lyndon's suicide attempt—the narrator tunes out diegetic sound (the lord's ghastly choking and the lady's piteous shrieks); in the first case he drily reads the lord's future obituary, and in the second he calmly informs us that Lady Lyndon has only swallowed enough poison to make herself grievously ill. Although this narrator never openly destroys the film's dramatic illusion, all of his deliberate foreshadowing implies a certain self-consciousness. Omniscient, prescient, and ironical, the narrator drives a wedge between the audience and events, and, through occasional remarks directly addressed to us, invites us to observe the story from his removed vantage point.

Several scholars have, however, rejected his invitation, claiming that this narrator is unreliable. Mark Crispin Miller, for example, argues with particular force against the narrator's trustworthiness.[16] I disagree and shall marshal my evidence to the contrary; yet as we shall see, the question of this narrator's reliability resists easy solution.

One frequently expressed misgiving about this narrator needs to be dismissed from the start. In light of the traditional critical aversion to redundancy, I am amused by the disturbance raised when Kubrick rather rigorously avoids overlapping the information given verbally and visually. This narrator tells us many things about Barry that the scenic presentation neither contradicts nor explicitly illustrates. However, if one is disposed to believe a narrator, whatever he says will be taken on faith, whereas if one already suspects him, divergent narration and image tracks only enlarge the opportunities for mistrust. In and of itself, the lack of simultaneous visual corroboration of a statement cannot be entered as evidence either way; we must look at the larger context.

This larger context includes judging whether the narrator's ironic stance and his treatment of the protagonist are in line with the norms of the film as a whole.

In many respects his distanced stance is substantiated by Kubrick's and cinematographer John Alton's use of the camera. Significantly, the film's first shot is an extreme long-shot of Barry's father being killed in a duel; the filmmakers further emphasize the camera's remove by placing it behind a low fence. Throughout the body of the film, they habitually employ two kinds of shots that reinforce our sense of detachment. The first of these is the reverse zoom: a shot will begin with a close-up of a detail—pistols being loaded, an inn sign, someone's face—and then the lens pulls back and back until the human figures are dwarfed by the landscape, a landscape that, as Richard

The camera waits as Barry and Nora approach in *Barry Lyndon*.

Schickel nicely puts it, "is as indifferent to the player's petty pursuits as he is impervious to its innocent charm." [17] The second technique, which is less blatant and has been overlooked by other critics, is found in such scenes as Nora and Barry's walk in the woods and Barry's first interview with the Chevalier: the camera is set up perhaps a hundred feet away from the characters and left to wait impassively, without moving or cutting away, as the characters approach it from the distance. At key moments, these patterns break—for example, the zoom *in* on Lady Lyndon during her first appearance, the handheld "involved" shots that capture the drawing-room brawl between Barry and Lord Bullingdon, the close-ups of Barry's face during his duel with Bullingdon—but for the most part the camerawork and composition are self-conscious, formal, and, above all, literally distancing.

The film's meticulous art direction also contributes to its cold tone. By means of careful choice of locations, detailed set dressing and props, painstaking placement of the actors and the camera, numerous shots are composed so as to resemble the paintings of eighteenth-century artists such as Hogarth, Gainsborough, and Constable. These static tableaux, these echoes of formal and timeless works of art, drain away the scenes' warmth or immediacy.

As for the central character, in the novel although we admire his physical courage and his attachment to his son, Barry proves to be a selfish, dishonorable, social-climbing rogue. Indisputably, Kubrick has softened Barry's personality: gone is his incessant bragging; gone are episodes that emphasized his fortune-hunting; gone is his emotional intimidation and physical abuse of

Stylized composition in *Barry Lyndon.*

Lady Lyndon. Kubrick's Barry is more loving to his wife, even more doting on his son, and he attains a certain nobility by sparing Bullingdon during the climactic duel invented by the director. Even the casting of pleasant and innocent-looking Ryan O'Neal (the only American amongst a European cast— Mark Crispin Miller aptly compares him with Henry James's Daisy Miller)[18] enlists audience sympathy. As William Stephenson remarks: "This Barry Lyndon is seen as a social outsider, that favorite figure of twentieth-century literature. He is a disadvantaged young man of the downtrodden Irish, exploited first by the warlords of continental Europe and later by a heartless English establishment."[19]

All of this notwithstanding, I find Miller's assertion that "Barry is not a scoundrel, but an innocent deprived of guidance" an overly sympathetic misreading, which leads him into rather tortured excuses for Barry's actions (and unfounded suspicions of the narrator).[20] Even if for argument's sake we temporarily disregard both *The Luck of Barry Lyndon* and the narrator's visually uncorroborated testimony, during the course of the film we see Barry put his hurt pride above Nora and her family's interests, desert from the British Army, steal a horse and uniform, lie and put on airs to Lischen, play toady to his Prussian superiors, work as a spy and then double-cross his employers, become a professional card-shark, marry Lady Lyndon for her money, neglect her and sleep with other women, alienate and beat his stepson, and squander his wife's fortune in hopes of purchasing a peerage. At times we are given or can deduce mitigating circumstances for this behavior, but if Barry is not an out-and-out blackguard, he is also something less than a lost sheep.

Miller believes that the narrator is unreliable because he "impute[s] base motives to a character who craves things far subtler than sexual gratification or wealth," and he labels the narrator's moralizing "jarringly intolerant." [21] But in fact, I believe that the narrator is neither particularly harsh towards Barry nor insensitive to moral ambiguities. The narrator does routinely reveal and ironically criticize unattractive aspects of Barry's personality; one typical instance occurs after Barry has stolen the officer's horse and uniform and deserted from the British Army. We see a long shot of Barry, garbed in this fine uniform, riding through peaceful countryside, while the narrator states: "Barry felt once more that he was in his proper sphere and determined never again to fall from the rank of a gentleman." But especially during the film's more somber second half, the narrator is very gentle on Barry, stressing Bullingdon's share of the quarrel, lingering over Barry's love for Bryan, commiserating over his final situation: "Utterly baffled and beaten, what was the lonely and broken-hearted man to do? He took the annuity and returned to Ireland. . . . He never saw Lady Lyndon again."

In all the discussions of the narrator's reliability, no one appears to have analyzed or given proper weight to exactly how Kubrick scripted the voiceover. The closer I look at this subject, the more I am convinced of the narrator's trustworthiness. Kubrick has not just invented the statements that reveal Barry's base motives and class pretensions out of thin air, but has lifted them almost precisely, with merely a change of pronouns, from the novel. Now and then Kubrick has selected a comment that is part of the (reliable) editor's footnotes and addenda, but for the most part, the information— whether damning or innocuous—comes from Barry's own mouth. Sometimes Kubrick has chosen a passage where the novel's narrator has been speaking with rare candor (for example, Barry's admission of his sense of freedom on leaving home for the first time and his recital of Lischen's previous amours). But in those frequent cases where Kubrick uses a sentence that originally inadvertently highlighted Barry's shortcomings, inevitably the passage takes on new meaning in its new context. In the novel, when Barry says:

> It would require a greater philosopher and historian than I am to explain the causes of the famous Seven Years' War in which Europe was engaged; and indeed, its origin has always appeared to me to be so complicated, and the books written about it so amazingly hard to understand, that I have seldom been much wiser at the end of a chapter than at the beginning,[22]

the reader catches the author's indirect satire of Barry's provincialism and ignorance. But when the film's narrator remarks over shots of a troopship at sea:

> It would require a great philosopher and historian to explain the causes of the famous Seven Years' War in which Europe was engaged and in which Barry's regiment was now on its way to take part,

the viewer takes this not as a statement of the narrator's inadequacies, but as an ironic judgment on the complicated and perhaps trivial causes of this conflict. In every case the move from novel to film is from unreliability and unconscious irony to reliability and conscious irony.

Nor can we leave out of consideration the sound of Michael Hordern's voice. Hordern, a British character actor then in his sixties, has often played the role of a world-weary political or military leader. His voice is kindly, confident, worldly, with no trace of self-importance or oiliness. The literary critic John Dodds has written of Thackeray: "The clue to his art is the complete and covering irony through which his view of life is filtered. It is an irony softened by a sad and wistful humanity, sharpened at times by an indignation against cant and affectation, but warmed also by the gentle melancholy that comes with the ironist's perception of the gap between man's aspirations and achievement."[23] This description also precisely fits the cinematic narrator, who indignantly punctures Barry's and others' affectations, but whose comments are colored by just this gentle melancholy. Surely this voice is the kindly, yet incessantly ironic, narrator of *Vanity Fair;* surely this is exactly what "Thackeray" sounds like.*

Although, here as elsewhere, intentionality should not be a major concern, I cannot believe that Kubrick set out to satirize "Thackeray." The director has remarked in interviews on his fondness for Thackeray in general and has compared his attraction to this novel to being in love with his wife.

The camerawork, the narrator's attitude towards the protagonist, the scripting of the voice-over, and the narrator's tone of voice all convince me that this narrator is honest and reliable, and that credence should be given to his statements even when corroboration by the scenic presentation is delayed, understated, or lacking. And yet . . . I admit to noticing certain tonal discrepancies between the narration and other aspects of the film. This narrator does not lie or mislead us, nor is he obviously naive or limited like Malick's narrators, but, somehow, something does not fit.

Michael Klein puts his finger on the difficulty sensed by every critic. He argues that the narrator is basically a reliable guide, but that two things are working against—or, more precisely, to one side of—the voice-over: the

---

*My identification of this narrator with "Thackeray" is so strong that I believe his area of responsibility extends beyond his oral commentary, i.e., that he is theoretically responsible for the bookish division of the film into two subtitled parts and for the printed epilogue. (This impression is heightened by Kubrick's selection of a pseudo-eighteenth-century typeface for these printed captions.) Unlike numerous other critics, I ascribe the equanimity, charity, and fatalism of the epilogue,

> It was in the reign of George III that the aforesaid personages lived and quarreled. Good or bad, handsome or ugly, rich or poor, they are all equal now,

to the narrator. The words—lifted from chapter 1 of the novel—are Thackeray's; the philosophy, vintage "Thackeray."

Lischen (lit by candlelight) in *Barry Lyndon.*

film's visual and musical splendor.[24] I mentioned earlier that the camera pulls back to distance the viewer from the petty proceedings, but the long-shots on which it finally rests are usually so stunning that the viewer becomes half lost in admiration. By the same token, several scenes are lit only by candlelight, and even when the warm, flickering light bathes scenes such as Barry lying in a drunken torpor, it elicits our involvement. And the characters' physical attractiveness and the sumptuousness of their costuming affect us deeply; we find it hard to accept the narrator's critical comments of someone who looks as pure as Lischen or as ingenuous as Barry. After all, *we are so used to believing that the camera does not lie,* we find it easier to start mistrusting the narrator. Even if, knowing that this film is about deceptive surfaces, we bring ourselves to accept his comments intellectually, willy-nilly our hearts become engaged.

The musical scoring adds extra complications. One of Kubrick's most notable strengths has always been his use of music, and he has loaded this film with stately baroque and classical pieces, selections from Vivaldi, Bach, Handel, and Schubert, and with careful arrangements of folk tunes. For the most part this music is used completely straightforwardly: Handel's dirgelike Sarabande is laid under the titles, the duels, and Bryan's funeral to create an atmosphere of pathos and doom, and Schubert's melancholy Piano Trio in E-flat Minor is assigned as Lady Lyndon's theme to speak for her about love,

loss, and despondency. Even when Kubrick makes the music comment ironically on the action—other critics have noticed the sly jibes in having four
drunken Englishmen in a bordello sing "The British Grenadiers" and in
choosing "Women of Ireland" as Nora's theme—the music is still emotionally charged and lends the scenes dignity. Each piece is repeated over and over
throughout the film, gathering associations with each new context, until the
viewer is enfolded in a web of stately poignancy.

The narrator/"Thackeray" is the voice of reason, morality, and kindliness,
but the extremes of emotion implied by the mise-en-scène and the music are
out of his province. Someone else is narrating this story, someone with less
easy confidence and less sense of humor, someone more calculating, someone
more willing to dignify these people and their sorrows, someone infinitely
more passionate. Kubrick has said revealingly· "The most important parts of
a film are the mysterious parts—beyond the reach of reason and language." [25]
"Thackeray" is trustworthy, but he is not the image-maker.

The resulting narrative discourse is fraught with tension. The viewer oscil-
lates between ironic detachment and empathy: Barry is both rogue and victim,
his difficulties both petty and sublimely tragic, his society both corrupt and
magnificent. Where one finally sets one's feet may depend on personal factors—how swayed one is by the music and scenic attractions, how disposed
one is to take a narrator seriously, how suspicious or how trusting one is of a
Thackerayan moral vantage point. But whatever choice one makes, the ironies
are irresolvable.

Irony is generally thought of as a mark of sophistication. D. C. Muecke
notes that it has pervaded twentieth-century literature, and that "nowadays
only popular literature is predominantly non-ironical." [26] To the extent that
voice-over contributes to film's potential for irony, it has been a factor in the
medium's "coming of age." It has helped film participate in what Scholes and
Kellogg judge as "one of the really developmental processes of [narrative]
history," to wit, "the growth of narrative artists' awareness of, and exploitation
of, the ironic possibilities inherent in the management of point of view." [27]

Yet I do not believe that in and of itself, irony accomplishes all that leftist
critics would wish in terms of making a text more open, more democratic.
Although irony can compromise the voice-over narrator, the ultimate authority for the text just moves back a level to the controlling image-maker.
This is certainly the case in *Barry Lyndon,* where devotees of the film explain
away the clash between the narrator and the scenic presentation by turning it
into a virtue—by seeing the film as "a triumphant display of life's ambiguities." The alternative for non-enthusiasts is to see the clash as a mistake, and
the film as an example of what happens when a director with unlimited control
loses perspective on his material's nuances. But note that if one embraces the
latter judgment, one still has not compromised the *image-maker,* one has in-

stead stepped out of the text altogether to criticize the flesh-and-blood *film-maker*. Image-makers, I think, are always reliable, always authoritative; rhetorical strategies for opening them up to criticism are just that—rhetorical strategies.

Wayne Booth has cautioned against the rather absurd tendency of modern critics to look for irony under every bush. But he has also noted that the "irony-hunt will go on. Once on this road we cannot turn back; we cannot pretend that things are as simple as they once seemed." [28] No form of story-telling is as simple as it once seemed, and it is this burden of self-consciousness about narrative voice that makes contemporary films with voice-over different from their forties predecessors. Compare the narration in such *noirs* as Michael Ritchie's *Fletch* (1985) or Ridley Scott's *Blade Runner* (1982) with the narration of *Double Indemnity;* compare the nostalgic narration of Rob Reiner's *Stand by Me* (1986) to that of *How Green Was My Valley.* In each case one finds a certain parodic element, a certain ironic self-detachment. The "telling" can never more be taken for granted: like it or not, it *is* part of the "show."

Conclusion

It is not insignificant that Robert Scholes and Robert Kellogg start their wide-ranging study of the nature of narrative with oral storytelling and end with film. Narrative cinema's roots spring from the same soil (fertilized by folktales, myths, epics, romances, histories, chronicles, and autobiographies) as those of the novel. When literary botanists such as Gérard Genette, Seymour Chatman, and Franz Stanzel study one species, it is hardly surprising that their findings are relevant to the other as well.

We might consider, too, that "narrative theory" itself is a product of the age of the cinema. Critics speculate as to how much Proust and all other twentieth-century novelists have been affected by photography and cinematography; I wonder whether Genette's thorough systemization of temporal order, duration, and frequency in *A la recherche du temps perdu* is not indebted to the fact that cinematic flashbacks and flashforwards have made temporal "anachronies" so concrete, so palpable. Surely the shift in terminology from "perspective" and "point of view" to "focalization," and the new conception of focalization as *moving in time,* testify to the cinema's influence on how we now think about narrative.

Small wonder, then, that we encountered no insurmountable difficulties in applying to film paradigms concerning irony, reliability, omniscience, epic situations, temporal relations between story and discourse, extent of the narrator's participation in his story, and narrative level. But the match is *not* perfect: careful adjustments need to be made in order to encompass the differences between, on the one hand, the literary implied author and narrator, and, on the other, the image-maker and voice-over narrator; and between an unbroken discourse of printed words and a discourse formed of light, shadow, color, music, sound, and oral language. We should never slight the fact that the cinema's bed is at the corner where narrative's garden touches the domains of drama, art, and technology.

As I have said, voice-over films are hybrids. The technique itself draws on two contradictory impulses—a hearkening back to simple oral storytelling and a modernist (if not "postmodernist") self-consciousness regarding narrative discourse. In any given film the scales can be tipped in either direction, but it may be that both are always present—that voice-over films turn Scholes and Kellogg's historical continuum of narrative forms into a circle.

Let me be quite clear: I do not believe that films that use the technique are necessarily "better"—aesthetically, politically, morally—than those that do not. To make such a claim would just be to substitute a new dogma in place of earlier prejudices that I have taken so many pains to dispel. A short time ago left-leaning critics castigated voice-over as repressive; I am suspicious of any sudden new rush to see it as politically progressive. Overtness of narrative discourse does not irresistibly imply honesty; self-reflexivity and self-consciousness do not necessarily compromise narrative authority. Sophisticated irony may add depth and provide a pleasant challenge, but it is not the only, or automatically the best, means of enriching a text, and it is not necessarily "liberating."

Yet there is no denying that the technique appeals to me, to the filmmakers who have used it so often, and to the moviegoing public. I trust that this study has demonstrated its usefulness in the grand cinematic tool chest, its facility in providing exposition, condensing time, motivating flashbacks, underscoring characters' flaws, parodying other texts, and so on. But the fact that the technique is useful does not account for its emotional appeal.

How does hearing a voice, as opposed to seeing an image or reading a title, affect us? Throughout his career of studying oral communication, Walter Ong, S. J., has stressed that sound creates a sense of connection. He argues that "by contrast with vision, the dissecting sense, sound is . . . a unifying sense. . . . The auditory ideal . . . is harmony, a putting together. . . . Because in its physical constitution as sound, the spoken word proceeds from the human interior and manifests human beings to one another as conscious interiors, as persons, the spoken word forms human beings into close-knit groups." [1] Ong is approaching the "psychodynamics of orality" from his position as a Jesuit priest, but interestingly enough, Mary Ann Doane's Lacanian speculations about the pleasure of hearing, which stress the infant's pleasure in its mother's soothing voice, make similar points about the voice's potential for creating an imaginary unity. [2] There seems to be widespread agreement about the voice's power to create a feeling of connection and intimacy.

This affective power is put to particular use in voice-over films. As noted earlier, voice-over serves to naturalize the strangeness of cinematic narration; an odd, impersonal narrative agency is thus humanized and tamed. To draw an analogy, the pleasure in hearing the image-maker speak is not far distinct from the pleasure in hearing computers talk. The wizards of high technology have grasped that no matter how "user-friendly" their printed instruction booklets and their programs are, they will only truly win over the technophobes when they add a voice. A voice does not trick one into believing that a computer is alive, or that it is a person, but what seemed alien now seems companionable. Marxist critics may be partially right in charging that in the case of both films and computers, such humanizing is a cynical fraud on the part of advanced capitalistic industries designed to lull consumers. Yet from another perspective, the adding of the voice, the anthropomorphization of the film or computer can be seen as merely a stripping away of an outer, technological shell to reveal the originating, *human* labor, intelligence, and creativity. "Huw Morgan" is not the real author of *How Green Was My Valley,* but as a human figure he is closer to Richard Llewellyn, Philip Dunne, Darryl Zanuck, Barbara McLean, John Ford et al. than are the camera, projector, and reels of celluloid.

Not only does the voice-over naturalize cinematic narration, as mentioned before, it also creates a special relationship with the viewer. The voice-over couches a film as a conscious, deliberate communication—which, in actuality, it is. Thus the narrator implicitly acknowledges the spectator's own existence and personhood; such an acknowledgement is a pleasant form of flattery. Moreover, because the cinematic story is now being consciously, deliberately displayed to the spectator, the spectator is placed less as a voyeur and more as an invited confidante. Since in many cases the voice-over allows the spectator—and the spectator alone—access to highly personal information, it thus simulates the exchange between the closest of friends or relations (except that in this instance the spectator is privy to another's secrets and not required to divulge any of his or her own). In sum, films that "speak" to us offer a close, mutually validating relationship; in religious terms, they forge an "I/Thou" bond.

Finally, and I think, most crucially, while we sit in darkened theaters, our attention focused on images larger than life, voice-over narration recreates our first experiences of narrative: being told a story, or being read aloud to. Not only does the technique hark back to the childhood of narrative art, it refers back to our own childhoods as well. The voice turns the moviegoing experience into Storytime.

We no longer gather around campfires or sit in Victorian parlors and listen to the latest installment of a Dickens novel; it is now extremely rare in adult lives to hear a story told out loud. Orson Welles once remarked on his "penchant for telling stories, like the Arab storytellers in the marketplaces." He continued: "I adore that. I never tire of hearing stories told, you know; so I commit the error of believing that everyone shares the same enthusiasm."[3] Those of us who share this enthusiasm, who never tire of hearing stories told, will never tire of the cinema's invisible storytellers.

Notes

Introduction

1. A recent exception is David Bordwell's *Narration in the Fiction Film* (Madison: Univ. of Wisconsin Press, 1985).

2. Seymour Chatman's *Story and Discourse: Narrative Structure in Fiction and Film* (Ithaca, N.Y.: Cornell Univ. Press, 1978) proves the rule, because Chatman includes film but doesn't give it equal attention.

3. See Bruce Kawin, *Mindscreen: Bergman, Godard, and First-Person Film* (Princeton, N.J.: Princeton Univ. Press, 1978).

4. William Labov, "The Transformation of Experience in Narrative Syntax," *Language in the Inner City: Studies in the Black English Vernacular* (Philadelphia: Univ. of Pennsylvania Press, 1972), pp. 354–96. I am indebted to Pratt (cited n. 5 below) for knowledge of Labov's work.

5. Mary Louise Pratt, *Toward a Speech Act Theory of Literary Discourse* (Bloomington: Indiana Univ. Press, 1977), pp. 38–78.

6. Jonathan Culler, *Structuralist Poetics: Structuralism, Linguistics and the Study of Literature* (Ithaca, N.Y.: Cornell Univ. Press, 1975), p. 203.

7. For an example of the confusion that results from lack of a clear definition, see Bernard F. Dick, *Anatomy of Film* (New York: St. Martin's Press, 1978), pp. 56–69.

8. Daniel Percheron, "Sound in Cinema and Its Relationship to Image and Diegesis," *Cinema/Sound,* Yale French Studies, 60 (1980), pp. 16–23.

9. Gérard Genette, *Narrative Discourse: An Essay in Method,* trans. Jane E. Lewin (Ithaca, N.Y.: Cornell Univ. Press, 1980).

1. The Prejudices against Voice-Over Narration

1. For early advocates of voice-over, see Alberto Cavalcanti, "Sound in Films," *Films* 1, no. 1 (Nov. 1939): 25–39; Gottfried Reinhardt, "Sound Track Narration: Its

Use Is Not Always a Resort of the Lazy and Incompetent," *Films in Review* 4, no. 9 (Nov. 1953): 459–60; William Seril, "Narration versus Dialogue: When Creatively Used, Both Aid the Visual Image," *Films in Review* 2, no. 7 (Aug.–Sep. 1951), 19–23. For contemporary defenders of voice-over, see Guido Fink, "From Showing to Telling: Off-Screen Narration in the American Cinema," *Letterature d'America* 3, no. 12 (Spring 1982): 5–37; and Eric Smoodin, "The Image and the Voice in the Film with Spoken Narration," *Quarterly Review of Film Studies* 8 (Fall 1983): 19–32. Most of my work on this study was completed before I read Fink's and Smoodin's articles; I have tried to indicate throughout areas in which we independently reach similar conclusions.

2. For a particularly clear discussion, see David A. Cook, *A History of Narrative Film* (New York: Norton, 1981), pp. 247–51, 254–57.

3. Rudolf Arnheim, "A New Laocoön," in *Film as Art* (Berkeley: Univ. of California Press, 1957), pp. 210–11.

4. Rick Altman, "Introduction," *Cinema/Sound*, Yale French Studies, 60 (1980), p. 14.

5. Susan Sontag, "Film and Theater," in *Film Theory and Criticism*, ed. Gerald Mast and Marshall Cohen (New York: Oxford Univ. Press, 1974), p. 252.

6. Sergei Eisenstein, "Statement on the Sound Film," in *Film Form*, ed. and trans. Jay Leyda (New York: Harcourt, Brace & World, 1949), p. 258.

7. Béla Balázs, *Theory of the Film: Character and Growth of a New Art*, trans. Edith Bone (New York: Dover, 1970), p. 44.

8. Arnheim, *Film as Art*, p. 229.

9. Siegfried Kracauer, *Theory of Film: The Redemption of Physical Reality* (London: Oxford Univ. Press, 1960), p. 104.

10. Hugo Munsterberg, *The Film: A Psychological Study*, excerpted in *Film Theory and Criticism*, ed. Mast and Cohen, p. 245.

11. W. J. T. Mitchell, *Iconology: Image, Text, Ideology* (Chicago: Univ. of Chicago Press, 1986).

12. Arnheim, *Film as Art*, p. iv.

13. Paul Rotha, *The Film Till Now*, with additional section by Richard Griffith (London: Spring Books, 1967), p. 406.

14. Christian Metz, *Film Language*, trans. Michael Taylor (New York: Oxford Univ. Press, 1974), p. 54.

15. Joseph M. Boggs, *The Art of Watching Films*, 2d ed. (Palo Alto, Calif.: Mayfield, 1985), p. 185.

16. Fink, "From Showing to Telling," p. 6.

17. Wayne Booth, *The Rhetoric of Fiction* (Chicago: Univ. of Chicago Press, 1961).

18. See Peter Wollen, *Signs and Meaning in the Cinema*, 3d ed. (Bloomington: Indiana Univ. Press, 1972), p. 122.

19. Umberto Eco, *A Theory of Semiotics* (Bloomington: Indiana Univ. Press, 1976).

20. Nelson Goodman, *Languages of Art* (Indianapolis: Hacket, 1976).

21. See Bill Nichols, *Ideology and the Image* (Bloomington: Indiana Univ. Press, 1981).

22. Roland Barthes, "The Rhetoric of the Image," in *Image/Music/Text*, trans. Stephen Heath (New York: Hill and Wang, 1977), pp. 38–41.

23. Robert Scholes and Robert Kellogg, *The Nature of Narrative* (London: Oxford Univ. Press, 1966), p. 280.

24. See, e.g., Edward Branigan, "Point of View in the Cinema: A Theory of Narration and Subjectivity in Classical Film" (Ph.D. diss., Univ. of Wisconsin, 1979), and Nick Browne, *The Rhetoric of Filmic Narration* (Ann Arbor, Mich.: UMI Research Press, 1983).

25. Brian Henderson, "Tense, Mood and Voice in Film (Notes after Genette)," *Film Quarterly* 36, no. 4 (Summer 1983): 16–17.

26. Sergei Eisenstein, "A Statement on the Sound Film," pp. 257–59.

27. Lee R. Bobker, *Elements of Film* (New York: Harcourt, Brace & World, 1969), p. 113.

28. Fink, "From Showing to Telling," p. 23.

29. "Say It with Narration," *Super-8 Filmmaker* (Jan./Feb. 1978): 28–32.

30. I. Watson, "The Technique Amateurs Should Make Their Own," *Movie Maker* 15 (Jan. 1981): 409–10.

31. Lillian Ross, *Picture* (New York: Rinehart, 1952).

32. Gerald Mast, *Howard Hawks, Storyteller* (New York: Oxford Univ. Press, 1982), pp. 338–43.

2. Ancestors, Influences, and Development

1. Charles Berg, "The Human Voice and the Silent Cinema," *Journal of Popular Film* 4, no. 2, (1975): 165–77, and Charles Musser, "The Nickelodeon Era Begins: Establishing the Framework for Hollywood's Mode of Representation," *Framework* 22/23 (Autumn 1983): 4–11.

2. Information on *benshi*s has been drawn from Noël Burch, *To The Distant Observer: Form and Meaning in the Japanese Cinema,* rev. and ed. Annette Michelson (Berkeley: Univ. of California Press, 1979); Joseph Anderson and Donald Richie, *The Japanese Film: Art and Industry* (Rutland, Vt: Charles E. Tuttle 1959); and Gerald Mast, *A Short History of the Movies,* 2d ed. (Indianapolis: Bobbs-Merrill, 1976), p. 446.

3. Quoted by Musser, "Nickelodeon Era," p. 8.

4. See William K. Everson, *American Silent Film* (New York: Oxford Univ. Press, 1978), pp. 126–41.

5. Iris Barry, *Let's Go to the Movies* (New York: Payson and Clarke, 1926), p. 78.

6. Vachel Lindsay, *The Art of the Moving Picture* (New York: Macmillan, 1922), p. xxix.

7. See Kevin Brownlow, *The Parade's Gone By* (Berkeley: Univ. of California Press, 1968), p. 294.

8. Erik Barnouw, *Handbook of Radio Production: An Outline of Studio Techniques and Procedures in the United States* (Boston: Little, Brown, 1949), p. 13.

9. Frank Buxton and Bill Owen, *The Big Broadcast,* rev. ed. (New York: Viking, 1972), p. 86.

10. Norm Corwin, "Sovereign Word: Some Notes on Radio Drama," *Theatre Arts* 24 (Feb. 1940): 130–36.

11. Erik Barnouw, *Handbook of Radio Writing: An Outline of Techniques and Markets in Radio Writing in the United States* (Boston: Little, Brown, 1939), pp. 50–51.

12. Jonathan Rosenbaum, "The Voice and the Eye: A Commentary on *The Heart of Darkness* Script," *Film Comment* 8, no. 4 (Nov.–Dec. 1972): 29.

13. James Naremore, *The Magic World of Orson Welles* (New York: Oxford Univ. Press, 1978), p. 21.

14. Felix Felton, *The Radio Play* (London: Sylvan Press, 1949) p. 86.

15. Max Wylie, *Radio Writing* (New York: Rinehart, 1939), pp. 72–73.

16. Archibald MacLeish, *The Fall of the City: A Verse Play for Radio* (New York: Farrar and Rinehart, 1937), p. xi.

17. *Variety,* 15 Jan. 1930, p. 21.

18. "Talking Shorts," *Variety,* 15 Jan. 1930, p. 22.

19. Raymond Fielding, *The American Newsreels, 1911–1967* (Norman: Univ. of Oklahoma Press, 1972), pp. 230–32.

20. As quoted by Raymond Fielding, *The March of Time, 1935–1951* (New York: Oxford Univ. Press, 1978), p. 240.

21. Lewis Jacobs, "From Innovation to Involvement," in *The Documentary Tradition* ed. Lewis Jacobs, 2d ed. (New York: Norton, 1979) pp. 75–76.

22. As quoted in James Curtis, *Between Flops: A Biography of Preston Sturges* (New York: Harcourt, Brace Jovanovich, 1982), p. 87.

23. Pauline Kael, "Raising Kane," *The Citizen Kane Book* (New York: Bantam, 1971), p. 51.

24. Letter to me from Philip Dunne, 3 Feb. 1983.

25. See Carl Dreher, "Recording, Re-recording, and Editing of Sound," *Journal of the Society of Motion Picture Engineers* 16, no. 6 (June 1931): 756–65.

26. Mary Ann Doane, "The Voice in the Cinema: The Articulation of Body and Space," *Cinema/Sound,* Yale French Studies, 60 (1980), p. 34.

27. Arthur Knight, *The Liveliest Art: A Panoramic History of the Movies* (New York: New American Library, 1957), p. 175.

28. Andrew Sarris, *The John Ford Movie Mystery* (Bloomington: Indiana Univ. Press, 1975), pp. 103–4.

29. Andrew Sarris, ed., *Interviews with Film Directors* (Indianapolis: Bobbs-Merrill, 1967), pp. 211–12, 460.

30. As quoted in John Dunning, *Tune in Yesterday* (Englewood Cliffs, N.J.: Prentice Hall, 1976), p. 459.

31. John Baxter, *Hollywood in the Sixties* (New York: A. S. Barnes, 1972), p. 11.

32. For discussions of voice-over in French films, see Alfred Guzzetti, *Two or Three Things I Know About Her: Analysis of a Film by Godard* (Cambridge, Mass.: Harvard Univ. Press, 1981); Annette Insdorf, *François Truffaut* (Boston: Twayne, 1978), pp. 90–94; Bettina Knapp, *Sacha Guitry* (Boston: Twayne, 1981); Nick Browne, "Film Form/Voice-Over: Bresson's *Diary of a Country Priest,*" *Cinema/Sound,* Yale French Studies, 60 (1980), pp. 233–40; and Marie-Claire Ropars-Wuilleumier, "The Disembodied Voice (*India Song*)," ibid., pp. 241–68.

33. See Jeffrey Youdelman, "Narration, Invention, and History," *Cinéaste* 12, no. 2 (Spring 1982): 8–15, and Bill Nichols, "The Voice of Documentary," *Film Quarterly* 36, no. 3 (Spring 1983): 17–30.

3. First-Person Narrators

1. Gérard Genette, *Narrative Discourse: An Essay in Method,* trans. Jane E. Lewin (Ithaca, N.Y.: Cornell Univ. Press, 1980), p. 244–45.

2. See Edward Branigan, "Point of View in the Cinema: A Theory of Narration and Subjectivity in Classical Film" (Ph.D. diss., Univ. of Wisconsin, 1979), pp. 83–87; Tony Pipolo, "The Aptness of Terminology: Point of View, Consciousness, and *Letter from an Unknown Woman,*" *Film Reader* 4 (1979): 166–68; and Ellen Feldman, "The Character-Centered Narrative: A Comparative Study of Three Films Structured According to the Organizing Perspective of a Single Character" (Ph.D. diss., New York Univ., 1981), p. 23.

3. Christian Metz, *Film Language,* trans. Michael Taylor (New York: Oxford Univ. Press, 1974), p. 21.

4. Bill Nichols, "The Voice of Documentary," *Film Quarterly* 36, no. 3 (Spring 1983): 18.

5. Nick Browne, introduction, *Film Reader* 4 (1979): 106.

6. Feldman, "The Character-Centered Narrative," p. 19.

7. Brian Henderson, "Tense, Mood, and Voice in Film (Notes after Genette)," *Film Quarterly* 36, no. 4 (Summer 1983): 6.

8. Eric Smoodin, "The Image and the Voice in the Film with Spoken Narration," *Quarterly Review of Film Studies* 8 (Fall 1983): 19.

9. For more on focalization, see Genette, *Narrative Discourse,* pp. 161–211, and Shlomith Rimmon-Kenan, *Narrative Fiction: Contemporary Poetics* (New York: Methuen, 1983), pp. 71–85.

10. See, for instance, Nick Browne, *The Rhetoric of Filmic Narration* (Ann Arbor, Mich.: UMI Research Press, 1982); Edward Branigan, "The Formal Permutations of the Point of View Shot," *Screen* 16, no. 3 (Autumn 1975), 54–64; Daniel Dayan, "The Tutor-Code of Classical Cinema," *Film Quarterly* 28, no. 1 (Fall 1974): 22–31; and William Rothman, "Against the System of Suture," *Film Quarterly* 29, no. 1 (Fall 1975): 45–50.

11. David Bordwell, *Narration in the Fiction Film* (Madison: Univ. of Wisconsin Press, 1985), p. 62.

12. Elizabeth W. Bruss, "Eye for I: Making and Unmaking Autobiography in Film," in *Autobiography: Essays Theoretical and Critical,* ed. James Olney (Princeton, N.J.: Princeton Univ. Press, 1980), p. 306.

13. Bertil Romberg, *Studies in the Narrative Technique of the First-Person Novel* (Stockholm: Almqvist and Wiksell, 1962), p. 33.

14. For more on the subject of fictional narratees in film see Guido Fink, "From Showing to Telling: Off-Screen Narration in the American Cinema," *Letterature d'America* 3, no. 12 (Spring 1982): 30–34.

15. See Laura Mulvey, "Visual Pleasure in Narrative Cinema," *Screen* 16 (Autumn 1975): 6–18, and E. Ann Kaplan, *Women and Film: Both Sides of the Camera* (New York: Methuen, 1983), pp. 23–35.

16. Romberg, p. 34.

17. Ibid., p. 33.

18. Metz, *Film Language,* p. 18.

19. Smoodin, "The Image and the Voice," pp. 22–24.

20. Michael Wood, "Movie Crazy," *New York Review of Books,* 29 Nov. 1973, p. 6.

21. As recounted in Philip Dunne, *Take Two: A Life in Movies and Politics* (New York: McGraw-Hill, 1980), pp. 91–103; letter to me from Philip Dunne, 3 Feb. 1983; and Mel Gussow, *Darryl F. Zanuck: Don't Say Yes Until I Finish Talking* (New York: Da Capo Press, 1980), p. 94.

22. As quoted in Gussow, *Zanuck,* p. 94.

23. Peter Bogdanovich, *John Ford* (Berkeley: Univ. of California Press, 1968), p. 107.

24. Telephone conversation with Barbara McLean, Feb. 1983.

25. Dunne's script of *How Green Was My Valley* was published in *Twenty Best Film Plays,* ed. John Gassner and Dudley Nichols (New York: Garland, 1943). However, as is my practice throughout this study, quotes are taken from the film, not the script.

26. J. A. Place, *The Non-Western Films of John Ford* (Secaucus, N.J.: Citadel Press, 1979), p. 172.

27. Henderson, "Tense, Mood, and Voice in Film," p. 11.

28. Walter Benjamin, *Illuminations,* ed. Hannah Arendt, trans. Harry Zohn (New York: Schocken Books, 1969), p. 92.

29. See also Tzvetan Todorov, "The Typology of Detective Fiction," in *The Poetics of Prose,* trans. Richard Howard (Ithaca, N.Y.: Cornell Univ. Press, 1977), pp. 42–52.

30. Mary Orr, "The Wisdom of Eve," *Cosmopolitan,* May 1946, pp. 72–75, 191–95.

31. Derek Conrad, "Putting on the Style," *Films and Filming* 6, no. 4 (Jan. 1960): 9.

32. Joseph Mankiewicz, *More About All About Eve: A Colloquy by Gary Carey with Joseph Mankiewicz* (New York: Random House, 1972), pp. 44–45, 98.

33. Mankiewicz's script is published in *More About All About Eve.* Yet there are subtle differences between the script and the film, and in all instances I have followed the film.

34. Mankiewicz, *More About All About Eve,* p. 57.

4. Third-Person Narrators

1. For another analysis that reaches this conclusion, see Carolyn Lee Reitz, "The Narrative Capabilities of Prose and Film" (Ph.D. diss., Univ. of Texas, Austin, 1978), pp. 199–205.

2. Noël Burch, *Theory of Film Practice,* trans. Helen R. Lane (New York: Praeger, 1973), pp. 26–27.

3. Franz Stanzel, *Narrative Situations in the Novel: Tom Jones, Moby Dick, The Ambassadors, Ulysses,* trans. James P. Pusack (Bloomington: Indiana Univ. Press, 1971), p. 43.

4. Seymour Chatman, *Story and Discourse: Narrative Structure in Fiction and Film* (Ithaca, N.Y.: Cornell Univ. Press, 1978), p. 212.

5. Pascal Bonitzer, "Les Silences de la voix," *Cahiers du Cinéma,* no. 256 (Feb./March 1975): 22–33.

6. Mary Ann Doane, "The Voice in the Cinema: The Articulation of Body and Space," *Cinema/Sound,* Yale French Studies, 60 (1980), p. 46.

7. Bill Nichols, "The Voice of Documentary," *Film Quarterly* 36, no. 3 (Spring 1983): 18.

8. Jeffrey Youdelman, "Narration, Invention and History," *Cinéaste* 12, no.2 (Spring 1982): 9.

9. William Lafferty, "A Re-appraisal of the 'Semi-Documentary' in Hollywood, 1945–1948," *Velvet Light Trap* 20 (Summer 1983): 22–26.

10. As related in Malvin Wald, afterword, *The Naked City: A Screenplay,* by Albert Maltz and Malvin Wald, ed. Matthew J. Bruccoli (Carbondale. Southern Illinois Univ. Press, 1979), 135–48; in Jim Bishop, *The Mark Hellinger Story: A Biography of Broadway and Hollywood* (New York: Appleton-Century-Crofts, 1952); and in a letter to me from Malvin Wald, 25 Feb. 1983. Direct quotes are from Wald's letter.

11. As quoted by Cynthia Grenier, "Interview with Jules Dassin," *Sight and Sound* 22, no. 3 (Winter 1957–58): 141.

12. Bosley Crowther, rev. of *The Naked City, New York Times,* 5 March 1948, p. 17.

13. The published screenplay is cited in n. 10 above. However, all quotations have been taken directly from the film.

14. Bonitzer, "Les Silences de la voix," p. 26. My translation.

15. Herb A. Lightman, "*The Naked City:* Tribute in Celluloid," *American Cinematographer* 29, no. 5 (May 1948): 152.

16. John McCarten, *New Yorker,* 13 March 1948, p. 80.

17. Bonitzer, "Les Silences de la voix," p. 26, trans. Mary Ann Doane and Sarah Kozloff.

18. Doane, "Voice in the Cinema," p. 42.

19. Ibid., p. 42.

20. Bonitzer, "Les Silences de la voix," pp. 24–25.

21. Mary Louise Pratt, *Toward a Speech Act Theory of Literary Discourse* (Bloomington: Indiana Univ. Press, 1977), pp. 101–6.

22. Susan Lanser, *The Narrative Act: Point of View in Prose Fiction* (Princeton, N.J.: Princeton Univ. Press, 1981), pp. 42–43.

23. Linda Dégh, *Folktales and Society: Storytelling in a Hungarian Peasant Community,* trans. Emily M. Schossberger (Bloomington: Indiana Univ. Press, 1969), p. 92.

24. See Laura Mulvey, "Visual Pleasure in Narrative Cinema," *Screen* 16 (Autumn 1975): 6–18, and E. Ann Kaplan, *Women And Film: Both Sides of the Camera* (New York: Methuen, 1983), pp. 23–35.

25. Molly Haskell, *From Reverence to Rape: The Treatment of Women in the Movies* (New York: Penguin Books, 1974), p. 7.

26. Ibid.

5. Irony in Voice-Over Films

1. Robert Scholes and Robert Kellogg, *The Nature of Narrative* (London: Oxford Univ. Press, 1966), pp. 277.

2. Claudia Gorbman, "Teaching the Soundtrack," *Quarterly Review of Film Studies* 1, no. 4 (Nov. 1976): 446.

3. Roland Barthes, "The Rhetoric of the Image," in *Image/Music/Text* trans. Stephen Heath (New York: Hill and Wang, 1977), pp. 32–51.

4. D. C. Muecke, *The Compass of Irony* (London: Methuen, 1969), p. 19.

5. Scholes and Kellogg, *Nature of Narrative,* pp. 52–53.

6. In the American cinema, Alfred Hitchcock's films perhaps come closest to questioning the silent image-maker's morality. For a thorough discussion of Hitchcock's self-consciousness, see William Rothman, *Hitchcock: The Murderous Gaze* (Cambridge, Mass.: Harvard Univ. Press, 1982).

7. For another discussion of the relation of irony to narrative level, see Shlomith Rimmon-Kenan, *Narrative Fiction: Contemporary Poetics* (New York: Methuen, 1983), p. 103.

8. See Bill Nichols, *Ideology and the Image* (Bloomington: Indiana Univ. Press, 1981), pp. 186–95.

9. Wayne Booth, *The Rhetoric of Fiction* (Chicago: Univ. of Chicago Press, 1961), p. 158.

10. Guido Fink, "From Showing to Telling: Off-Screen Narration in the American Cinema," *Letterature d'America* 3, no. 12 (Spring 1982): 24.

11. See Kristin Thompson, "The Duplicitous Text: An Analysis of *Stage Fright,*" *Film Reader* 2 (1977): 52–64.

12. Mary Louise Pratt, *Toward a Speech Act Theory of Literary Discourse* (Bloomington: Indiana Univ. Press, 1977), p. 170.

13. As quoted by Beverly Walker, "Malick on *Badlands,*" *Sight and Sound* 44, no. 2 (Spring 1975): 82.

14. Richard Schickel, "Kubrick's Greatest Gamble," *Time,* 15 Dec. 1975, pp. 72–78.

15. There are several lengthy and perceptive studies of *Barry Lyndon* to which I am indebted in a general sense. See Thomas Allen Nelson, *Kubrick: Inside a Film Artist's Maze* (Bloomington: Indiana Univ. Press, 1982), pp. 165–96; William Stephenson, "The Perception of 'History' in Kubrick's *Barry Lyndon,*" *Film/Literature Quarterly* 9, no. 4 (1981); and Robert Kolker, *A Cinema of Loneliness: Penn, Kubrick, Coppola, Scorsese, Altman* (New York: Oxford Univ. Press, 1980), pp. 124–38.

16. Mark Crispin Miller, "*Barry Lyndon* Reconsidered," *Georgia Review* 30, no. 4 (Winter 1976): 827–53.

17. Schickel, "Kubrick's Greatest Gamble," p. 76.

18. Miller, "*Barry Lyndon* Reconsidered," p. 845.

19. Stephenson, "The Perception of 'History' in Kubrick's *Barry Lyndon,*" p. 253

20. Miller, "*Barry Lyndon* Reconsidered," p. 830.

21. Ibid., pp. 829–30.

22. William Makepeace Thackeray, *The Luck of Barry Lyndon,* ed. Martin F. Anisman (New York: New York Univ. Press, 1970); p. 116.

23. John W. Dodds, "Thackeray's Irony," in *Thackeray: A Collection of Critical Essays,* ed. Alexander Welsh (Englewood Cliffs, N.J.: Prentice-Hall, 1968), p. 33.

24. Michael Klein, "Narrative and Discourse in Kubrick's Modern Tragedy," in *The English Novel and the Movies*, ed. Michael Klein and Gillian Parker (New York: Ungar, 1981), pp. 95–107.

25. As quoted by John Hofsess, "How I Learned to Stop Worrying and Love *Barry Lyndon*," *New York Times*, 11 Jan. 1976, sec. 2, p. 13.

26. Muecke, *Compass of Irony*, p. 10.

27. Scholes and Kellogg, *Nature of Narrative*, p. 241.

28. Booth, *Rhetoric of Fiction*, p. 369.

Conclusion

1. Walter J. Ong, *Orality and Literacy: The Technologizing of the Word* (New York: Methuen, 1982), pp. 72, 74.

2. Mary Ann Doane, "The Voice in the Cinema: The Articulation of Body and Space," *Cinema/Sound*, Yale French Studies, 60 (1980), pp. 43–46.

3. As quoted in Maurice Bessy, *Orson Welles*, trans. Ciba Vaughan (New York: Crown, 1971), p. 113.

Filmography

This is a list of roughly four-hundred English-language feature films that use voice-over narration, whether first person or third, primary or embedded. It includes those that rely heavily on the technique and those that use it only minimally for a prelude or an isolated embedded story. It is hardly a complete listing of every title that has ever used the technique: the best one can hope for is that it is representative. Thus, rather than restrict it only to films that I have seen myself, and slant it towards my personal viewing history and access to archives, I have relied on a large and varied group of informants and on published sources. Despite my best efforts at double-checking, the decision to rely on informants introduces the possibility of inaccuracy; since memories concerning voice-over can be hazy, a few of the films listed below may not actually use the technique, but rely instead on a related strategy, such as interior monologue or flashbacks without voice-over. I believe, however, that what the filmography loses in absolute surety, it gains in providing a more comprehensive and balanced survey.

The rationale for compiling such a list was to illustrate how very large a role voice-over has played in American cinema, to see if any patterns emerge, and to aid any future researchers into this topic. Unscientific though it may be, patterns do indeed appear. While glancing at it, readers are invited to note the wide spectrum of genres, but the preponderance of adaptations, *noirs*, semi-documentaries, war films, epics, and domestic comedies; the frequent appearance of certain directors (not only Welles, Wilder, Allen, and Huston, but such studio workhorses as Curtiz and Minnelli); and the chronological distribution.

The 1930s

Forgotten Commandments (1932), Gasnier and Schorr
The Power and the Glory (1933), William Howard
The Bride of Frankenstein (1935), James Whale
Gold Is Where You Find It (1938), Michael Curtiz

1939

Confessions of a Nazi Spy, Anatole Litvak
Juarez, William Dieterle
The Roaring Twenties, Raoul Walsh
Stanley and Livingstone, Henry King
Wuthering Heights, William Wyler

1940

All This and Heaven Too, Anatole Litvak
Kitty Foyle, Sam Wood
The Mummy's Hand, Christy Cabanne
North West Mounted Police, Cecil B. De Mille
One Million B.C., Hal Roach and Hal Roach, Jr.
Our Town, Sam Wood
Pinocchio, Walt Disney
Rebecca, Alfred Hitchcock
Swiss Family Robinson, Edward Ludwig
Waterloo Bridge, Mervyn LeRoy

1941

Cheers for Miss Bishop, Tay Garnett
Citizen Kane, Orson Welles
The 49th Parallel, Michael Powell
H. M. Pullman, Esq., King Vidor
Hold Back the Dawn, Mitchell Leisen
How Green Was My Valley, John Ford
The Lady Eve, Preston Sturges
The Road to Zanzibar, Victor Schertzinger
Tobacco Road, John Ford
A Woman's Face, George Cukor

1942

The Ghost of Frankenstein, Erle Kenton
The Great Man's Lady, William Wellman
The Hard Way, Vincent Sherman
In Which We Serve, Noel Coward and David Lean
Journey Into Fear, Norman Foster (and Orson Welles)
The Magnificent Ambersons, Orson Welles
The Moon and Sixpence, Albert Lewin
Now Voyager, Irving Rapper
Random Harvest, Mervyn LeRoy
To Be or Not to Be, Ernst Lubitsch
Yankee Doodle Dandy, Michael Curtiz

1943

Action in the North Atlantic, Lloyd Bacon
Casablanca, Michael Curtiz
Crash Dive, Archie Mayo
Guadalcanal Diary, Lewis Seiler
Heaven Can Wait, Ernst Lubitsch
The Human Comedy, Clarence Brown
I Walked with a Zombie, Jacques Tourneur
Mission to Moscow, Michael Curtiz
The More the Merrier, George Stevens
So Proudly We Hail, Mark Sandrich
The Uninvited, Lewis Allen

1944

The Bridge of San Luis Rey, Rowland Lee
Christmas Holiday, Robert Siodmak
The Conspirators, Jean Negulesco
Double Indemnity, Billy Wilder
Dragon Seed, Jack Conway and Harold Bucquet
Guest in the House, John Brahm
Henry V, Laurence Olivier
Jane Eyre, Robert Stevenson
The Lady and the Monster, George Sherman
Laura, Otto Preminger
The Mask of Dimitrios, Jean Negulesco
Murder, My Sweet, Edward Dmytryk
Passage to Marseille, Michael Curtiz
The Seventh Cross, Fred Zinnemann
Since You Went Away, John Cromwell
The Story of Dr. Wassell, Cecil B. De Mille
Summer Storm, Douglas Sirk
The Whistler, William Castle

1945

Back to Bataan, Edward Dmytryk
Dead of Night, Alberto Cavalcanti and Charles Crichton
House on 92nd Street, Henry Hathaway
I Know Where I'm Going, Michael Powell and Emeric Pressburger
Mildred Pierce, Michael Curtiz
Notorious Gentleman, Sidney Gilliat
Objective Burma!, Raoul Walsh
The Picture of Dorian Gray, Albert Lewin
Pride of the Marines, Delmer Daves
Roughly Speaking, Michael Curtiz

The Seventh Veil, Compton Bennett
The Southerner, Jean Renoir
Spellbound, Alfred Hitchcock
The Story of G.I. Joe, William Wellman
A Tree Grows in Brooklyn, Elia Kazan
The Valley of Decision, Tay Garnett

1946

Brief Encounter, David Lean
Detour, Edgar Ulmer
Gilda, Charles Vidor
Great Expectations, David Lean
Green for Danger, Sidney Gilliat
It's a Wonderful Life, Frank Capra
The Killers, Robert Siodmak
The Locket, John Brahm
Margie, Henry King
Night Editor, Henry Levin
The Postman Always Rings Twice, Tay Garnett
The Razor's Edge, Edmund Goulding
The Secret Heart, Robert Leonard
13 Rue Madeleine, Henry Hathaway
To Each His Own, Mitchell Leisen

1947

Blind Spot, Robert Gordon
Boomerang, Elia Kazan
The Brasher Doubloon, John Brahm
Brute Force, Jules Dassin
Crossfire, Edward Dmytryk
Dead Reckoning, John Cromwell
Duel in the Sun, King Vidor
The Fugitive, John Ford
Golden Earrings, Mitchell Leisen
Kiss of Death, Henry Hathaway
The Long Night, Anatole Litvak
Monsieur Verdoux, Charles Chaplin
Mother Wore Tights, Walter Lang
My Favorite Brunette, Elliott Nugent
Nora Prentiss, Vincent Sherman
Out of the Past, Jacques Tourneur
Possessed, Curtis Bernhardt
The Senator Was Indiscreet, George Kaufman
The Unconquered, Cecil B. De Mille
The Unfaithful, Vincent Sherman

1948

Berlin Express, Jacques Tourneur
Call Northside 77, Henry Hathaway
The Dark Past, Rudolph Maté
The Emperor Waltz, Billy Wilder
Enchantment, Irving Reis
Force of Evil, Abraham Polonsky
Hamlet, Laurence Olivier
High Wall, Curtis Bernhardt
I Remember Mama, George Stevens
The Inside Story, Allan Dwan
Joan of Arc, Victor Fleming
The Lady from Shanghai, Orson Welles
Letter from an Unknown Woman, Max Ophuls
Mr. Blandings Builds His Dream House, H.C. Potter
The Naked City, Jules Dassin
The Pirate, Vincente Minnelli
Raw Deal, Anthony Mann
Red River, Howard Hawks
The Search, Fred Zinnemann
The Secret Beyond the Door, Fritz Lang
Street with No Name, William Keighley
T-Men, Anthony Mann
Walk a Crooked Mile, Gordon Douglas

1949

All the King's Men, Robert Rossen
Beyond the Forest, King Vidor
Border Incident, Anthony Mann
The Bribe, Robert Z. Leonard
Chicago Deadline, Lewis Allen
City across the River, Maxwell Shane
Criss Cross, Robert Siodmak
Flamingo Road, Michael Curtiz
The Great Gatsby, Elliott Nugent
In the Good Old Summertime, Robert Leonard
Kind Hearts and Coronets, Robert Hamer
A Letter to Three Wives, Joseph Mankiewicz
Madame Bovary, Vincente Minnelli
One Woman's Story, David Lean
Reign of Terror, Anthony Mann
A Run for Your Money, Charles Frend
Sands of Iwo Jima, Allan Dwan
She Wore a Yellow Ribbon, John Ford
The Snake Pit, Anatole Litvak

Task Force, Delmer Daves
Under Capricorn, Alfred Hitchcock
The Undercover Man, Joseph Lewis

1950

All About Eve, Joseph Mankiewicz
Between Midnight and Dawn, Gordon Douglas
Broken Arrow, Delmer Daves
Cheaper by the Dozen, Walter Lang
Father of the Bride, Vincente Minnelli
The Glass Menagerie, Irving Rapper
Madeleine, David Lean
The Men, Fred Zinnemann
Night and the City, Jules Dassin
Side Street, Anthony Mann
Stage Fright, Alfred Hitchcock
Sunset Boulevard, Billy Wilder
The Wild Heart, Michael Powell and Emeric Pressburger
The Woman in Question, Anthony Asquith

1951

Across the Wide Missouri, William Wellman
An American in Paris, Vincente Minnelli
Captain Horatio Hornblower, Raoul Walsh
Decision before Dawn, Anatole Litvak
Father's Little Dividend, Vincente Minnelli
Hollywood Story, William Castle
House on Telegraph Hill, Robert Wise
I Was a Communist for the FBI, Gordon Douglas
The Man in the White Suit, Alexander MacKendrick
Quo Vadis, Mervyn LeRoy
The Red Badge of Courage, John Huston
The River, Jean Renoir
Scrooge/A Christmas Carol, Brian Hurst

1952

The Bad and the Beautiful, Vincente Minnelli
Bend of the River, Anthony Mann
The Big Sky, Howard Hawks
The First Time, Frank Tashlin
It's a Big Country, Charles Vidor, Richard Thorpe, John Sturges, Don Hartman, Don
     Weis, Clarence Brown, and William Wellman
The Marrying Kind, George Cukor
One Minute to Zero, Tay Garnett

Plymouth Adventure, Clarence Brown
The Quiet Man, John Ford
Ruby Gentry, King Vidor
Singin' in the Rain, Stanley Donen and Gene Kelly
Snows of Kilimanjaro, Henry King

1953

The Band Wagon, Vincente Minnelli
City That Never Sleeps, John Auer
The Desert Rats, Robert Wise
Glen or Glenda, Edward Wood, Jr.
Island in the Sky, William Wellman
Little Boy Lost, George Seaton
Niagara, Henry Hathaway
Stalag 17, Billy Wilder

1954

Animal Farm, John Halas and Joy Batchelor
The Barefoot Contessa, Joseph Mankiewicz
Loophole, Harold Schuster
Romeo and Juliet, Renato Castellani
Salt of the Earth, Herbert Biberman
Susan Slept Here, Frank Tashlin
Woman's World, Jean Negulesco

1955

Battle Cry, Raoul Walsh
Doctor at Sea, Ralph Thomas
The French They Are a Funny Race, Preston Sturges
Hell's Island, Phil Karlson
Killer's Kiss, Stanley Kubrick
Land of the Pharaohs, Howard Hawks
Mr. Arkadin, Orson Welles
The Sea Chase, John Farrow
The Seven Year Itch, Billy Wilder
Three Cases of Murder, Wendy Toye
To Hell and Back, Jesse Hibbs

1956

Godzilla, Terry Morse
High Society, Charles Walters
Invasion of the Body Snatchers, Don Siegel
The Killing, Stanley Kubrick

The Lieutenant Wore Skirts, Frank Tashlin
Miracle in the Rain, Rudolph Maté
Moby Dick, John Huston
Nightmare, Maxwell Shane
The Searchers, John Ford
The Solid Gold Cadillac, Richard Quine

1957

Beau James, Meville Shavelson
The Incredible Shrinking Man, Jack Arnold
Love in the Afternoon, Billy Wilder
Paths of Glory, Stanley Kubrick
Peyton Place, Mark Robson
The Spirit of St. Louis, Billy Wilder

1958

Cinerama's South Seas Adventure, Frances Lyon
Lafayette Escadrille, William Wellman
No Time for Sergeants, Mervyn LeRy
The Old Man and the Sea, John Sturges
The Vikings, Richard Fleisher

1959

Ben Hur, William Wyler
Journey to the Center of the Earth, Henry Levin
Operation Petticoat, Blake Edwards
Plan Nine from Outer Space, Edward Wood, Jr.

1960

The Apartment, Billy Wilder
Bells are Ringing, Vincente Minnelli
The Last Voyage, Andrew Stone
Spartacus, Stanley Kubrick
Town without Pity, Gottfried Reinhardt

1961

All in a Night's Work, Joseph Anthony
El Cid, Anthony Mann
King of Kings, Nicholas Ray
One Two Three, Billy Wilder
X-15, Richard Donner

1962

Freud: The Secret Passion, John Huston
How the West Was Won, Henry Hathaway, John Ford, George Marshall
Lolita, Stanley Kubrick
The Man Who Shot Liberty Valance, John Ford
Mr. Hobbs Takes a Vacation, Henry Koster
The Pigeon That Took Rome, Melville Shavelson
To Kill a Mockingbird, Robert Mulligan
The Trial, Orson Welles

1963

Cleopatra, Joseph Mankiewicz
P.T. 109, Leslie Martinson
Tom Jones, Tony Richardson

1964

Cheyenne Autumn, John Ford
Dr. Strangelove, Stanley Kubrick
The Fall of the Roman Empire, Anthony Mann
36 Hours, George Seaton
Zulu, Cy Endfield

1965

The Amorous Adventures of Moll Flanders, Terence Young
Cat Ballou, Elliot Silverstein
The Family Jewels, Jerry Lewis
Faster Pussycat! Kill! Kill!, Russ Meyer
Ghengis Kahn, Henry Levin
The Hallelujah Trail, John Sturges
Those Magnificent Men in Their Flying Machines, Ken Annakin

1966

The Bible, John Huston
Falstaff (Chimes at Midnight), Orson Welles
What's Up, Tiger Lily?, Woody Allen

1967

The Big Mouth, Jerry Lewis
The St. Valentine's Day Massacre, Roger Corman

1968

Arizona Bushwackers, Lesley Selander
The Night They Raided Minsky's, William Friedkin
Romeo and Juliet, Franco Zeffirelli
Star, Robert Wise

1969

Castle Keep, Sydney Pollack
MacKenna's Gold, J. Lee Thompson
The Reivers, Mark Rydell
Sinful Davey, John Huston
Take the Money and Run, Woody Allen

1970

Little Big Man, Arthur Penn
The Private Life of Sherlock Holmes, Billy Wilder
Start the Revolution without Me, Bud Yorkin

1971

A Clockwork Orange, Stanley Kubrick
Evel Knievel, Marvin Chomsky
The Go-Between, Joseph Losey
Summer of '42, Robert Mulligan

1972

Bad Company, Robert Benton
Jeremiah Johnson, Sydney Pollack
The Life and Times of Judge Roy Bean, John Huston
Santee, Gary Nelson
Silent Running, Douglas Trumbull

1973

Badlands, Terence Malick
Blume in Love, Paul Mazursky
F for Fake, Orson Welles

1974

Blazing Saddles, Mel Brooks
The Great Gatsby, Jack Clayton

1975

Barry Lyndon, Stanley Kubrick
Bugs Bunny, Superstar, Larry Jackson
Farewell, My Lovely, Dick Richards
Love and Death, Woody Allen
The Man Who Would Be King, John Huston

1976

Taxi Driver, Martin Scorsese

1977

Annie Hall, Woody Allen
Islands in the Stream, Franklin Schaffner
Julia, Fred Zinnemann
Providence, Alain Resnais

1978

The Boys in Company C, Sidney Furie
Days of Heaven, Terence Malick
Fedora, Billy Wilder
International Velvet, Brian Forbes
Lord of the Rings, Ralph Bakshi

1979

Apocalypse Now, Francis Ford Coppola
The Jerk, Carl Reiner
Manhattan, Woody Allen
Real Life, Albert Brooks
Starting Over, Alan Pakula

1980

The Big Red One, Sam Fuller
The Gods Must Be Crazy, Jamie Uys
Stardust Memories, Woody Allen

1981

Chariots of Fire, Hugh Hudson
The Chosen, Jeremy Kagan
Four Friends, Arthur Penn

History of the World, Part I, Mel Brooks
The Legend of the Lone Ranger, William Fraker
My Dinner with André, Louis Malle
Tarzan, The Ape Man, John Derek

1982

Blade Runner, Ridley Scott
Cannery Row, David Ward
Chan Is Missing, Wayne Wang
Chilly Scenes of Winter, Joan M. Silver
Conan the Barbarian, John Milius
Dark Crystal, Jim Henson
Dead Men Don't Wear Plaid, Carl Reiner
Evil Under the Sun, Guy Hamilton
Frances, Graeme Clifford
Hammett, Wim Wenders
Missing, Constantin Costa-Gavras
My Favorite Year, Richard Benjamin
The Road Warrior, George Miller
Sophie's Choice, Alan Pakula
Star Trek II: The Wrath of Kahn, Nicholas Meyer
The Sword and the Sorcerer, Albert Pyun

1983

A Christmas Story, Bob Clark
Deal of the Century, William Friedkin
Heat and Dust, James Ivory
Never Cry Wolf, Carroll Ballard
The Outsiders, Francis Ford Coppola
The Right Stuff, Philip Kauffman
Risky Business, Paul Brickman
Testament, Lynne Littman
Trenchcoat, Michael Tuchner
Twilight Zone—The Movie, Steven Spielberg, John Landis, Joe Dante, and George
    Miller
The Year of Living Dangerously, Peter Weir
Zelig, Woody Allen

1984

Blood Simple, Joel and Ethan Cohen
The Bounty, Roger Donaldson
Broadway Danny Rose, Woody Allen
Children of the Corn, Fritz Kiersch
Gremlins, Joe Dante

Ice Pirates, Stewart Raffill
Johnny Dangerously, Amy Heckerling
Once Upon a Time in America, Sergio Leone
Star Trek III: The Search for Spock, Leonard Nimoy
Windy City, Armyan Bernstein

1985

Enemy Mine, Wolfgang Petersen
Fletch, Michael Ritchie
Hannah and Her Sisters, Woody Allen
Kiss of the Spider Woman, Hector Babenco
Mishima: A Life in Four Chapters, Paul Schrader
The Name of the Rose, Jean-Jacques Annaud
Out of Africa, Sydney Pollack
Rustler's Rhapsody, Hugh Wilson
Young Sherlock Holmes, Barry Levinson

1986

Absolute Beginners, Julian Temple
The Clan of the Cave Bear, Michael Chapman
Dreamchild, Gavin Millar
Mosquito Coast, Peter Weir
Platoon, Oliver Stone
She's Gotta Have It, Spike Lee
Stand by Me, Rob Reiner
True Stories, David Bryne

1987

Gardens of Stone, Francis Ford Coppola
Radio Days, Woody Allen
Raising Arizona, Joel Cohen

Bibliography of Works Cited

Altman, Rick. "Introduction." *Cinema/Sound*. Yale French Studies, 60 (1980), pp. 3–15.

Anderson, Joseph, and Donald Richie. *The Japanese Film: Art and Industry*. Rutland, Vt. Charles E. Tuttle, 1959.

Arnheim, Rudolf. *Film as Art*. Berkeley: Univ. of California Press, 1957.

Balázs, Béla. *Theory of the Film: Character and Growth of a New Art*. Trans. Edith Bone. New York: Dover, 1970.

Barnouw, Erik. *Handbook of Radio Production: An Outline of Studio Techniques and Procedures in the United States*. Boston: Little, Brown, 1949.

———. *Handbook of Radio Writing: An Outline of Techniques and Markets in Radio Writing in the United States*. Boston: Little, Brown, 1939.

Barry, Iris. *Let's Go to the Movies*. New York: Payson and Clarke, 1926.

Barthes, Roland. "The Rhetoric of the Image." In *Image/Music/Text,* trans. Stephen Heath, pp. 32–51. New York: Hill and Wang, 1977.

Baxter, John. *Hollywood in the Sixties*. New York: A. S. Barnes, 1972.

Benjamin, Walter. *Illuminations*. Ed. Hannah Arendt; trans. Harry Zohn. New York: Schocken Books, 1969.

Berg, Charles. "The Human Voice and the Silent Cinema." *Journal of Popular Film* 4, no. 2 (1975): 165–77.

Bessy, Maurice. *Orson Welles*. Trans. Ciba Vaughan. New York: Crown, 1971.

Bishop, Jim. *The Mark Hellinger Story: A Biography of Broadway and Hollywood*. New York: Appleton-Century-Crofts, 1952

Bluestone, George. *Novels into Film: The Metamorphosis of Fiction into Film*. Berkeley: Univ. of California Press, 1957.

Bobker, Lee R. *Elements of Film*. New York: Harcourt, Brace & World, 1969.

Bogdanovich, Peter. *John Ford*. Berkeley: Univ. of California Press, 1968.

Boggs, Joseph M. *The Art of Watching Films*. 2d ed. Palo Alto, Calif.: Mayfield, 1985.

Bonitzer, Pascal. "Les Silences de la voix." *Cahiers du Cinéma,* no. 256 (Feb./March 1975): 22–33. Reprinted in *Narrative, Apparatus, Ideology,* ed. Philip Rosen, pp. 319–34. New York: Columbia Univ. Press, 1986.

Booth, Wayne. *The Rhetoric of Fiction.* Chicago: Univ. of Chicago Press, 1961.

Bordwell, David. *Narration in the Fiction Film.* Madison: Univ. of Wisconsin Press, 1985.

Branigan, Edward. "The Formal Permutations of the Point of View Shot." *Screen* 16, no. 3 (Autumn 1975): 54–64.

———. "Point of View in the Cinema: A Theory of Narration and Subjectivity in Classical Film." Ph.D. diss., Univ. of Wisconsin, 1979.

Browne, Nick. "Film Form/Voice-Over: Bresson's *Diary of a Country Priest.*" *Cinema/Sound.* Yale French Studies, 60 (1980), pp. 233–40.

———. "Introduction." *Film Reader* 4 (1979): 105–7.

———. *The Rhetoric of Filmic Narration.* Ann Arbor, Mich.: UMI Research Press, 1982.

Brownlow, Kevin. *The Parade's Gone By.* Berkeley: Univ. of California Press, 1968.

Bruss, Elizabeth W. "Eye for I: Making and Unmaking Autobiography in Film." In *Autobiography: Essays Theoretical and Critical,* ed. James Olney, pp. 296–320. Princeton, N.J.: Princeton Univ. Press, 1980.

Burch, Noël. *Theory of Film Practice.* Trans. Helen R. Lane. New York: Praeger, 1973.

———. *To the Distant Observer: Form and Meaning in the Japanese Cinema.* Rev. and ed. Annette Michelson. Berkeley: Univ. of California Press, 1979.

Butterfield, Fox. "TV Returns to Vietnam to Dissect the War." *New York Times,* 2 Oct. 1983, sec. 2, pp. 1, 37.

Buxton, Frank and Bill Owen. *The Big Broadcast.* Rev. ed. New York: Viking, 1972.

Carroll, Lewis. *Through the Looking Glass.* In *The Annotated Alice,* ed. Martin Gardner. New York: Clarkson N. Potter, 1960.

Cavalcanti, Alberto, "Sound in Films." *Films* 1, no. 1 (1939): 25–39.

Chatman, Seymour. *Story and Discourse: Narrative Structure in Fiction and Film,* Ithaca, N.Y.: Cornell Univ. Press, 1978.

Conrad, Derek. "Putting on the Style." *Films and Filming* 6, no. 4 (1960): 9, 33.

Cook, David. *A History of Narrative Film.* New York: Norton, 1981.

Corwin, Norman. "Sovereign Word: Some Notes on Radio Drama." *Theatre Arts* 24 (1940): 130–36.

Crowther, Bosley. Rev. of *The Naked City. New York Times,* 5 March 1948, p. 17.

Curtis, James. *Between Flops: A Biography of Preston Sturges.* New York: Harcourt, Brace Jovanovich, 1982.

Dayan, Daniel. "The Tutor-Code of Classical Cinema." *Film Quarterly* 29, no. 1 (1974): 22–31.

Dégh, Linda. *Folktales and Society: Storytelling in an Hungarian Peasant Community.* Trans. Emily M. Schossberger. Bloomington: Indiana Univ. Press, 1969.

Dick, Bernard. *Anatomy of Film.* New York: St. Martin's Press, 1978.

Doane, Mary Ann. "The Voice in the Cinema: The Articulation of Body and Space." *Cinema/Sound,* Yale French Studies, 60 (1980), pp. 33–50. Reprinted in *Narrative, Apparatus, Ideology,* ed. Philip Rosen, pp. 335–48. New York: Columbia Univ. Press, 1986.

Dodds, John. "Thackeray's Irony." In *Thackeray: A Collection of Critical Essays*, ed. Alexander Welsh. Englewood Cliffs, N.J.: Prentice-Hall, 1968.

Dreher, Carl. "Recording, Re-recording and Editing of Sound." *Journal of the Society of Motion Picture Engineers* 16, no. 6 (1931): 756–65.

Dunne, Philip. Letter to the author. 3 Feb. 1983.

————. *Take Two: A Life in Movies and Politics*. New York: McGraw-Hill, 1980.

Dunning, John. *Tune in Yesterday*. Englewood Cliffs, N.J.: Prentice-Hall, 1976.

Eco, Umberto. *A Theory of Semiotics*. Bloomington: Indiana Univ. Press, 1976.

Eisenstein, Sergei. *Film Form*. Ed. and trans. Jay Leyda. New York: Harcourt, Brace & World, 1949.

Everson, William K. *American Silent Film*. New York: Oxford Univ. Press, 1978.

Feldman, Ellen. "The Character-Centered Narrative: A Comparative Study of Three Films Structured According to the Organizing Perspective of a Single Character." Ph.D. diss, New York Univ., 1981.

Felton, Felix. *The Radio Play*. London: Sylvan Press, 1949.

Fielding, Raymond. *The American Newsreels, 1911–1967*. Norman: Univ. of Oklahoma Press, 1972.

————. *The March of Time, 1935–1951*. New York: Oxford Univ. Press, 1978.

Fink, Guido. "From Showing to Telling: Off-Screen Narration in the American Cinema." *Letterature d'America* 3, no. 12 (1982): 5–37.

Genette, Gérard. *Narrative Discourse: An Essay in Method*. Trans. Jane E. Lewin. Ithaca, N.Y.: Cornell Univ. Press, 1980.

Giannetti, Louis D. *Understanding Movies*. 2d ed. Englewood Cliffs, N.J.: Prentice-Hall, 1976.

Goldman, William. *Adventures in the Screen Trade*. New York: Warner, 1983.

Goodman, Nelson. *Languages of Art*. Indianapolis: Hacket, 1976.

Gorbman, Claudia. "Teaching the Soundtrack." *Quarterly Review of Film Studies* 1, no. 4 (1976): 446–52.

Grenier, Cynthia. "Interview with Jules Dassin." *Sight and Sound* 22, no. 3 (1957–58): 141–43.

Gussow, Mel. *Don't Say Yes Until I Finish Talking: A Biography of Darryl F. Zanuck*. Garden City, N.Y.: Doubleday, 1971. Reprinted as *Darryl F. Zanuck: Don't Say Yes Until I Finish Talking*. New York: Da Capo Press, 1980.

Guzzetti, Alfred. *Two or Three Things I Know About Her: Analysis of a Film by Godard*. Cambridge, Mass.: Harvard Univ. Press, 1981.

Haskell, Molly. *From Reverence to Rape: The Treatment of Women in the Movies*. New York: Penguin Books, 1974.

Henderson, Brian. "Tense, Mood, and Voice in Film (Notes after Genette)." *Film Quarterly* 36, no. 4 (1983): 4–17.

Hofsess, John. "How I Learned to Stop Worrying and Love *Barry Lyndon*." *New York Times*, 11 Jan. 1976, sec. 2, p. 13.

Insdorf, Annette, *François Truffaut*. Boston: Twayne, 1978.

Kael, Pauline. "Raising Kane." In *The Citizen Kane Book*, pp. 2–124. New York: Bantam, 1971.

Kaplan, E. Ann. *Women and Film: Both Sides of the Camera*. New York: Methuen, 1983.

Kawin, Bruce. *Mindscreen: Bergman, Godard, and First-Person Film.* Princeton, N.J.: Princeton Univ. Press, 1978.

Klein, Michael. "Narrative and Discourse in Kubrick's Modern Tragedy." In *The English Novel and the Movies,* ed. Michael Klein and Gillian Parker, pp. 95–107. New York: Ungar, 1981.

Knapp, Bettina. *Sacha Guitry.* Boston: Twayne, 1981.

Knight, Arthur. *The Liveliest Art: A Panoramic History of the Movies.* New York: New American Library, 1957.

Kolker, Robert. *A Cinema of Loneliness: Penn, Kubrick, Coppola, Scorsese, Altman.* New York: Oxford Univ. Press, 1980.

Kracauer, Siegfried. *Theory of Film: The Redemption of Physical Reality.* London: Oxford Univ. Press, 1960.

Labov, William. "Transformation of Experience in Narrative Syntax." In *Language in the Inner City: Studies in the Black English Vernacular,* pp. 354–96. Philadelphia: Univ. of Pennsylvania Press, 1972.

Lafferty, William. "A Re-appraisal of the Hollywood 'Semi-Documentary,' 1945–1948." *Velvet Light Trap* 20 (Summer 1983): 22–26.

Lanser, Susan. *The Narrative Act: Point of View in Prose Fiction.* Princeton, N.J.: Princeton Univ. Press, 1981.

Lightman, Herb A. "*The Naked City:* Tribute in Celluloid." *American Cinematographer* 29, no. 5 (1948): 152–53, 178–79.

Lindsay, Vachel. *The Art of the Moving Picture.* New York: Macmillan, 1922.

Llewellyn, Richard. *How Green Was My Valley.* New York: Macmillan, 1940.

McCarten, John. Rev. of *The Naked City. New Yorker,* 13 March 1948, p. 80.

McLean, Barbara. Telephone interview by the author. Feb. 1983.

MacLeish, Archibald. *The Fall of the City: A Verse Play for Radio.* New York: Farrar and Rinehart, 1937.

Mankiewicz, Joseph. *More About All About Eve: A Colloquy by Gary Carey with Joseph L. Mankiewicz.* New York: Random House, 1972.

Mast, Gerald. *Howard Hawks, Storyteller.* New York: Oxford Univ. Press, 1982.

———. *A Short History of the Movies.* 2d ed. Indianapolis: Bobbs-Merrill, 1976.

Metz, Christian. *Film Language.* Trans. Michael Taylor. New York: Oxford Univ. Press, 1974.

Miller, Mark Crispin. "*Barry Lyndon* Reconsidered." *Georgia Review* 30, no. 4 (1976): 827–53.

Mitchell, W. J. T. *Iconology: Image, Text, Ideology.* Chicago: Univ. of Chicago Press, 1986.

Muecke, D. C. *The Compass of Irony.* London: Methuen, 1969.

Mulvey, Laura. "Visual Pleasure in Narrative Cinema." *Screen* 16 (1975): 6–18.

Musser, Charles. "The Nickelodeon Era Begins: Establishing the Framework for Hollywood's Mode of Representation." *Framework* 22/23 (1983): 4–11.

Naremore, James. *The Magic World of Orson Welles.* New York: Oxford Univ. Press, 1978.

Nelson, Thomas Allen. *Kubrick: Inside a Film Artist's Maze.* Bloomington: Indiana Univ. Press, 1982.

Nichols, Bill. *Ideology and the Image.* Bloomington: Indiana Univ. Press, 1981.

———. "The Voice of Documentary." *Film Quarterly* 36, no. 3 (1983): 17–30.

Ong, Walter J. *Orality and Literacy: The Technologizing of the Word.* New York: Methuen, 1982.

Orr, Mary. "The Wisdom of Eve." *Cosmopolitan,* May 1946, pp. 72–75, 191–195.

Percheron, Daniel. "Sound in Cinema and its Relationship to Image and Diegesis." *Cinema/Sound,* Yale French Studies, 60 (1980), pp. 16–23.

Pipolo, Tony. "The Aptness of Terminology: Point of View, Consciousness and *Letter from an Unknown Woman." Film Reader* 4 (1979): 166–74.

Pratt, Mary Louise. *Toward A Speech Act Theory of Literary Discourse.* Bloomington: Indiana Univ. Press, 1977.

Reinhardt, Gottfried. "Sound Track Narration: Its Use Is Not Always a Resort of the Lazy and Incompetent." *Films in Review* 4, no. 9 (1953): 459–60.

Reitz, Carolyn Lee. "The Narrative Capabilities of Prose and Film." Ph.D. diss., Univ. of Texas, Austin, 1978.

Rimmon-Kenan, Shlomith. *Narrative Fiction: Contemporary Poetics.* New York: Methuen, 1983.

Romberg, Bertil. *Studies in the Narrative Technique of the First-Person Novel.* Stockholm: Almquist and Wiksell, 1962.

Ropars-Wuillemier, Marie-Claire. "The Disembodied Voice (*India Song*)." *Cinema/Sound,* Yale French Studies, 60 (1980), pp. 241–68.

Rosenbaum, Jonathan. "The Voice and the Eye: A Commentary on the *Heart of Darkness* Script." *Film Comment* 8, no. 4 (1972): 27–32.

Ross, Lillian. *Picture.* New York: Rinehart, 1952.

Rotha, Paul. *The Film Till Now.* With additional section by Richard Griffith. London: Spring Books, 1967.

Rothman, William. "Against the System of Suture." *Film Quarterly* 29, no. 1 (1975): 45–50.

———. *Hitchcock: The Murderous Gaze.* Cambridge, Mass.: Harvard Univ. Press, 1982.

Sarris, Andrew, ed. *Interviews with Film Directors.* Indianapolis: Bobbs-Merrill, 1967.

———. *The John Ford Movie Mystery.* Bloomington: Indiana Univ. Press, 1975.

"Say It with Narration." *Super-8 Filmmaker* 6 (1978): 28–32.

Schickel, Richard. "Kubrick's Greatest Gamble." *Time,* 15 Dec. 1975, pp. 72–78.

Scholes, Robert, and Robert Kellogg. *The Nature of Narrative.* London: Oxford Univ. Press, 1966.

Seril, William. "Narration versus Dialogue: When Creatively Used, Both Aid the Visual Image." *Films in Review* 2, no. 7 (1951): 19–23.

Smoodin, Eric. "The Image and the Voice in the Film with Spoken Narration." *Quarterly Review of Film Studies* 8 (Fall 1983): 19–32.

Stanzel, Franz. *Narrative Situations in the Novel: Tom Jones, Moby Dick, The Ambassadors, Ulysses.* Trans. James P. Pusack. Bloomington: Indiana Univ. Press, 1971.

Stephenson, William. "The Perception of 'History' in Kubrick's *Barry Lyndon." Film/Literature Quarterly* 9, no. 4 (1981): 251–60.

"Talking Shorts." *Variety,* 15 Jan. 1930, p. 22.

Thackeray, William Makepeace. *The Luck of Barry Lyndon.* Ed. Martin F. Anisman. New York: New York Univ. Press, 1970.

Thompson, Kristin. "The Duplicitous Text: An Analysis of *Stage Fright." Film Reader* 2 (1977): 52–64.

Todorov, Tzvetan. "The Typology of Detective Fiction." In *The Poetics of Prose,* trans. Richard Howard, pp. 42–52. Ithaca, N.Y.: Cornell Univ. Press, 1977.

Wald, Malvin. Afterword. *The Naked City: A Screenplay,* by Albert Maltz and Malvin Wald. Ed. Matthew J. Bruccoli. Carbondale: Southern Illinois Univ. Press, 1979.

————. Letter to the author. 25 Feb. 1983.

Walker, Beverly. "Malick on *Badlands.*" *Sight and Sound* 44, no. 2 (1975): 82–83.

Watson, I. "The Technique Amateurs Should Make Their Own." *Movie-Maker* 15 (1981): 409–10.

Watts, Richard, Jr. *New York Herald Tribune,* 17 Aug. 1933, sec. 1, p. 12.

Wollen, Peter. *Signs and Meaning in the Cinema.* 3d ed. Bloomington: Indiana Univ. Press, 1972.

Wood, Michael. "Movie Crazy." *New York Review of Books,* 29 Nov. 1973, pp. 6–10.

Wylie, Max. *Radio Writing.* New York: Rinehart, 1939.

Youdelman, Jeffrey. "Narration, Invention, and History: A Documentary Dilemma." *Cinéaste* 12, no. 2 (1982): 8–15.

Index

Note: In the case of films and novels having the same title, the citations below refer to films unless otherwise specified.

Compositor:	G & S Typesetters, Inc.
Text:	10/12 Times Roman
Display:	Helvetica
Printer:	Braun-Brumfield, Inc.
Binder:	Braun-Brumfield, Inc.